"More desirable than gold... and sweeter than honey..."

That's what Psalm 19 says about Bible truths—
the same rich truths presented just for kids
in Questar's **Gold'n'Honey Books**

Gold 'n'
Honey
BOOKS

QUESTAR PUBLISHERS, INC.
SISTERS, OREGON

THE BEGINNER'S
ABC BIBLE MEMORY BOOK

© 1992 by V. Gilbert Beers

Cover Design by Bruce DeRoos

PRINTED IN THE UNITED STATES OF AMERICA

International Standard Book Number: 0-945564-41-4

The Beginner's
ABC
Bible Memory
Book

text by **V. GILBERT BEERS**
Illustrated by **C. SPENCER MORRIS**

Why Memorize Bible Verses?

Why bother? Why take the trouble to memorize verses? My wife Arlie and I have memorized dozens of Bible verses throughout our lifetimes. We've also helped our children memorize dozens of verses. But what's the point of doing all this work?

Here are a dozen *delightful* reasons to memorize Bible verses:

1. **TO KEEP US FROM SIN.** How many of us have been severely tempted, then we remember a Bible verse that we memorized years before? It was enough to throw a stop sign before us. Somehow it's much more difficult to go ahead with temptation when a key Bible verse stares us in the face.

2. **TO REINFORCE A BIBLE TRUTH.** We are studying the Bible, looking for a key truth. Suddenly a verse flashes before us. We memorized it long ago. It brings to a burning focus the truth we need.

3. **TO HELP US DELIGHT IN THE WONDERS OF GOD'S WORLD.** We are traveling through beautiful scenery. Suddenly a Bible verse comes to mind. The wonders of God's world around us come alive with rich new meaning.

4. **TO HELP US WORSHIP GOD.** We are in church. Or in camp. Or at a retreat. Or wandering on a lonely shore. We are reaching out to God to worship Him. A verse comes to mind. We think of Him. We worship Him.

5. **TO COMFORT US IN TIMES OF TROUBLE.** Trouble comes from everywhere. We all face it. It's suddenly there. We have no time to look up verses in a concordance. Then a verse we learned comes to mind. It brings great comfort to a fearful heart.

6. **TO SHOW US WHAT GOD WANTS.** Should we take this job or stay where we are? Should we make this choice? What should we do? We all stand at crossroads, dozens of times. What does God want us to do? We'll be glad to do it, if only He will tell us. A verse comes to mind. Another follows. God's Word is there to give us help.

7. **TO HELP OTHERS.** A friend or neighbor faces a tough problem. We want to help. Our words seem shallow. Then a Bible verse comes to mind. We quote it or we put it into our own words. God's wisdom shows forth.

8. **TO WITNESS TO OTHERS.** Someone asks why we do what we do. Why are we different? It is an opportunity to witness about Jesus. But there is no time to search a concordance. There isn't even a Bible nearby. But you have Bible verses stored in your head and heart. As they come to mind, you have something significant to say.

9. **TO HELP US PRAY.** We are alone in our room. Or we are driving to work. Or we could be almost anywhere. We are concerned about someone or something. We begin to pray. A Bible verse comes to mind. Then another. God's Word helps us pray as we should.

10. **TO HELP US TEACH.** Somewhere along the way we each take time to teach. We'll be glad for each Bible verse we learned as we share God's Word with others. How those verses enrich our teaching!

11. **TO ENRICH WHAT OTHERS TEACH US.** A teacher teaches. A preacher preaches. A Bible study leader speaks. An idea is born. A truth emerges. An application is made. You remember a Bible verse to enrich that truth. How glad you are!

12. **TO REINFORCE GREAT HYMNS.** How often as we sing a great hymn a Bible verse comes to mind! When it does, it enriches that hymn and highlights our time of worship.

The Most Memorized Verse of All

Of all Bible verses, the most memorized is John 3:16. It is the heart of the Gospel—God's plan of salvation — in one simple statement.

Before going any further, perhaps you and your child would like to memorize this beautiful verse in your favorite Bible version.

For God so loved the world, that he gave his only begotten Son, that whosoever believeth in him should not perish, but have everlasting life. *(King James Version)*

For God so loved the world that He gave His only begotten Son, that whoever believes in Him should not perish but have everlasting life. *(New King James Version)*

For God loved the world so much that he gave his only Son so that anyone who believes in him shall not perish but have eternal life. *(The Living Bible)*

For God so loved the world that he gave his one and only Son, that whoever believes in him shall not perish but have eternal life. *(New International Version)*

Which Version Should I Use?

The Bible verses you memorize will last a lifetime. They will go with you wherever you go. They will guide you when all other voices fade. But how do you know which version to use?

To help you make that decision, and it is your decision to make, we have included key verses in four widely used versions. Putting memory verses in all four versions will let you to see them side by side, and thus it will help you decide which version you would like to use.

Choosing a Bible version is a personal matter. All four versions included here are accurate. So are other versions we could have included, if space had permitted. But some versions will speak more personally to you than others. Choose your memory version carefully. It will be with you for a lifetime.

Throughout this book the Bible versions will be identified with the following abbreviations: KJV *(King James Version)*, NKJV *(New King James Version)*, TLB *(The Living Bible)*, and NIV *(New International Version)*.

God bless you as you and your child (or student) enjoy more and more of the benefits that come with memorizing Scripture!

—V. Gilbert Beers

The Best Way to Use This Book

1. Read the story that begins each chapter, noting the featured Bible teachings that are indicated by words set in all capital letters.

2. When you reach a page that looks like this, explore what the Bible has to say about the teaching presented in the chapter.

3. Study the Bible memory technique that is provided under a heading like this one.

4. Now you're ready to begin learning some of the Scripture verses referred to here!

What the Bible Says about Anger

Here are three important Bible teachings about ANGER.

CONTROL YOUR ANGER.
—*Proverbs 14:29*

ANSWER ANGRY WORDS WITH KIND ONES.
—*Proverbs 15:1*

YOU ARE WISE WHEN YOU CONTROL YOUR ANGER.
—*Proverbs 29:11*

Would you like to memorize one of these important teachings? Or perhaps you would like to memorize a Bible verse about one of them? Allison will help you.

Allison's Way to Memorize a Bible Verse

Allison wants to help Andrew and you learn at least one good Bible verse about ANGER.

Do you see the Bible teachings about ANGER above? Do you see the Bible verse where each teaching is found? Choose a verse that you would like to memorize. Now find that verse in the box on page 19. Choose the version you like best.

Read the verse ten times to yourself. Then read it to someone else, like your mother or father. Now try to say it to that person without reading it. Keep doing this until you have memorized it.

17

Note to readers: You will also probably want to become familiar with these features in the back of the book:

- **26 Ways to Memorize Bible Verses**—*page 273*
- **The Top 50** (the most often memorized Bible memory verses)—*page 278*
- **Memory Plus** (more Bible-memory ventures)—*page 281*
- **Bible Memory Topics** (an alphabetized list of all the topics featured in the book, along with Bible references)—*page 282*

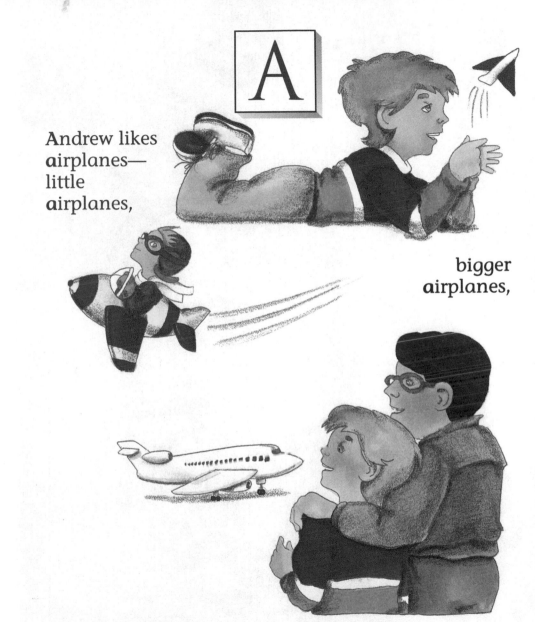

Andrew likes airplanes—little airplanes,

bigger airplanes,

and the biggest airplanes at the airport.

Allison is an artist—
she likes to draw,
she likes to color,
she likes to paint.

But Allison does NOT
like to play with airplanes.

This makes Andrew
ANGRY at Allison.

"Watch your ANGER, Andrew," Allison tells him.
So Allison told Andrew this story:

Andrew's Airplanes

One day Andrew wanted to play with his airplanes. But he wanted someone to play with him.

"Will you play airplanes with me?" Andrew asked his friend Alex.

"Thank you, Andrew," said Alex. "But I promised Mother I would be home soon. Would you like to come to my house to play?"

Andrew was ANGRY at Alex because he would not do what he asked.

"No, I will never go to your house to play!" Andrew shouted.

"You shouldn't get so ANGRY," said Alex. "You won't have many friends if you get so ANGRY at them."

Andrew knew that was true. "But what can I do to keep from being so ANGRY?" he thought.

Andrew called his friend Allan.

"I want to play airplanes," he told Allan. "Will you play airplanes with me?"

"I'm sorry, Andrew," said Allan. "I'd like to, but I promised Mother I would clean my room."

Andrew was ANGRY at Allan because he would not do what he asked. "Then don't ask me to play with you again," he shouted.

"You shouldn't get so ANGRY," said Allan. "You won't have many friends if you get so ANGRY at them."

Andrew knew this was true. "But what can I do to keep from getting so ANGRY?" he thought.

Andrew asked his sister Allison next. "Will you play airplanes with me?" he asked.

"You know I do not like to play airplanes," said Allison. "I know you don't like to paint and draw with me. So I don't ask you to do that."

Andrew became ANGRY at Allison. He said some things that weren't very nice.

"You shouldn't get so ANGRY," said Allison. "You won't have many friends if you get so ANGRY at them."

Andrew knew this was true. "But what can I do to keep from getting so ANGRY?" he asked.

"CONTROL YOUR ANGER," said Allison. "The Bible says so. There are good verses in the Bible about ANGER. They will help you remember not to get ANGRY at your friends."

Andrew thought about his ANGER. He thought about what his friends had said. He did not want to lose his friends.

"I would like to learn what God says about CONTROLLING MY ANGER," said Andrew. "Can you help me find some good Bible verses? Maybe I can learn one now."

Do you see where Andrew found the Bible verse about ANGER?

What the Bible Says about Anger

Here are three important Bible teachings about ANGER.

> **CONTROL YOUR ANGER**
> —*Proverbs 14:29*
>
> **ANSWER ANGRY WORDS WITH KIND ONES**
> —*Proverbs 15:1*
>
> **YOU ARE WISE WHEN YOU CONTROL YOUR ANGER**
> —*Proverbs 29:11*

Would you like to memorize one of these important teachings? Or perhaps you would like to memorize a Bible verse about one of them? Allison will help you.

Allison's Way to Memorize a Bible Verse

Allison wants to help Andrew and you learn at least one good Bible verse about ANGER.

Do you see the Bible teachings about ANGER above? Do you see the Bible verse where each teaching is found? Choose a verse that you would like to memorize. Now find that verse in the box on page 19. Choose the version you like best.

Read the verse ten times to yourself. Then read it to someone else, like your mother or father. Now try to say it to that person without reading it. Keep doing this until you have memorized it.

Why should you control your ANGER?

Because God says you should.

Because your friends will like you better.

Because this will make your parents happy.

Because you will be happy if you do.

PROVERBS 14:29

He that is slow to wrath is of great understanding. *(King James Version)*

He who is slow to wrath has great understanding. *(New King James Version)*

A wise man controls his temper. *(The Living Bible)*

A quick-tempered man displays folly. *(New International Version)*

PROVERBS 15:1

A soft answer turneth away wrath; but grievous words stir up anger. *(KJV)*

A soft answer turns away wrath, but a harsh word stirs up anger. *(NKJV)*

A soft answer turns away wrath, but harsh words cause quarrels. *(TLB)*

A gentle answer turns away wrath, but a harsh word stirs up anger. *(NIV)*

PROVERBS 29:11

A fool uttereth all his mind; but a wise man keepeth it in till afterwards. *(KJV)*

A fool vents all his feelings, but a wise man holds them back. *(NKJV)*

A rebel shouts in anger; a wise man holds his temper in and cools it. *(TLB)*

A fool gives full vent to his anger, but a wise man keeps himself under control. *(NIV)*

PSALM 34:13

> Keep thy tongue from evil, and thy lips from speaking guile. *(KJV)*

> Keep your tongue from evil, and your lips from speaking guile. *(NKJ)*

> Then watch your tongue! Keep your lips from lying. *(TLB)*

> Keep your tongue from evil and your lips from speaking lies. *(NIV)*

PROVERBS 21:23

> Whoso keepeth his mouth and his tongue keepeth his soul from troubles. *(KJV)*

> Whoever guards his mouth and tongue keeps his soul from troubles. *(NKJ)*

> Keep your mouth closed and you'll stay out of trouble. *(TLB)*

> He who guards his mouth and his tongue keeps himself from calamity. *(NIV)*

MATTHEW 15:18

> But those things which proceed out of the mouth come forth from the heart; and they defile the man. *(KJV)*

> But those things which proceed out of the mouth come from the heart, and they defile a man. *(NKJ)*

> But evil words come from an evil heart, and defile the man who says them. *(TLB)*

> But the things that come out of the mouth come from the heart, and these make a man unclean. *(NIV)*

B

Bart likes to build things—

he builds houses,

he builds ladders,

and he builds other things.

21

Bart uses tools to build things.
Sometimes he uses a saw.
Sometimes he uses a screwdriver.
And sometimes he uses a hammer.

But sometimes Bart doesn't use a tool well.
When this happens, Bart often says some
BAD WORDS.

Friends like Brad do not like Bart's BAD WORDS.
"Be careful," said Brad. "BAD WORDS are bad when
you say them. They are also bad when we hear
them." So Brad told Bart this story:

Bart the Builder

Bart is a builder. He likes to build things with wood. Bart saws the wood. He hammers nails into it. He puts screws in it with his screwdriver. Sometimes Bart uses his tools well. And sometimes he doesn't! That's when Bart uses BAD WORDS.

"**BAD WORDS** make **B**art sound like a bad **b**oy,"
said **B**rent. "But **B**art is not a bad **b**oy."

"I don't want to sound like a bad **b**oy," **B**art said
to his friend **B**rent. "But what can I do to stop using
BAD WORDS?"

Bart tried to stop using **BAD WORDS**. But before long he dropped a big **b**oard on his foot. Ouch! Bart said some more **BAD WORDS**. **B**art's friend **B**etty heard what he said. But **B**etty did not like **B**art's **BAD WORDS**.

"BAD WORDS make Bart sound like a bad boy,"
said Betty. "But Bart is not a bad boy."

"I don't want to sound like a bad boy," Bart said
to his friend Betty. "But what can I do to stop using
BAD WORDS?"

Bart tried to stop using **B**AD WORDS again.
Then the playhouse he built fell down. It became a
pile of **b**oards. **B**art said some **B**AD WORDS again.

This time **B**art's friend **B**rad heard what he said.
Brad did not like **B**art's **B**AD WORDS.

"**B**AD WORDS make **B**art sound like a bad boy," said **B**rad. "But **B**art is not a bad **b**oy."

"I don't want to sound like a bad **b**oy," **B**art said to his friend **B**rad. "But what can I do to stop using BAD WORDS?"

"God has some GOOD WORDS for you in the **B**ible," said **B**rad. "These GOOD WORDS will help you not to use BAD WORDS. Then you will not sound like a bad **b**oy."

"I would like to learn some of God's GOOD WORDS," **B**art said. "Will you help me find these GOOD WORDS?"

Here is an important truth from the **B**ible: GOD'S GOOD WORDS WILL KEEP YOU FROM USING BAD WORDS.

What the Bible Says about
Good Words and Bad Words

Here are three important Bible teachings about GOOD WORDS and BAD WORDS.

WATCH WHAT YOU SAY
—Psalm 34:13

DON'T SAY THINGS THAT WILL GET YOU INTO TROUBLE
—Proverbs 21:23

BAD WORDS SHOW A PERSON'S BAD HEART
—Matthew 15:18

Brad's Way to Learn
a Bible Verse

Brad wants to help Bart and you learn a Bible verse about GOOD WORDS and BAD WORDS. Or, you may want to learn two or three or even more.

Do you see the Bible teachings above? Do you see the Bible verse where each teaching is found? Choose a verse you would like to memorize. Now find that verse in the box on page 20. Choose the version you like best.

Say the first two words of this verse five times. Now say the next three words of this verse five times. Now say all five words together five times. Do you know them? Keep doing this until you have memorized the verse. Be sure to learn the reference, too.

Which of these are true?

BAD WORDS make you sound like a bad person.

BAD WORDS make Jesus sad.

BAD WORDS are dirty, like falling in the mud.

Chad likes clocks. He often visits the Clock Shop downtown. The Clock Shop man likes to show Chad his clocks.

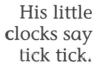

His little clocks say tick tick.

His middle-size clocks say tick tock.

And his big clocks say tock tock.

One day Chad had a little talk with his Clock Shop friend. "I don't know what to CHOOSE," said Chad. "On Sunday morning I want to go to church and Sunday School. But my friends want me to go with them. I don't like what these friends do. But I do want friends. What should I do?"

The Clock Shop man told Chad this story:

Chad's Choices

Once there was a boy named Chad. He liked to go to church and Sunday School. He learned good things from the Bible. He learned about Jesus. Chad and Jesus became good friends.

Chad had other friends. They did not want him to go to church and Sunday School. They wanted him to do other things with them on Sunday morning. But the things they did would not please God.

Chad sat on a bus-stop bench near the Clock Shop. He couldn't decide what to do. How could he CHOOSE? Then he saw his friend, the Clock Shop man, inside. Chad went in to talk with him.

"How can I CHOOSE between two things to do?" Chad asked the Clock Shop man. "Look at it this way," answered the Clock Shop man. "You really are CHOOSING between two ways to live. You are CHOOSING betweenGod's Way and your other friends' wrong way."

The Clock Shop man picked up a clock. "IT IS ALWAYS THE RIGHT TIME TO CHOOSE GOD'S WAY," he said. "It is never the right time to CHOOSE the wrong way. So which way should you CHOOSE?"

When the Clock Shop man finished the story, Chad looked puzzled. "But who can help me CHOOSE the right way?"

"Ask God to help you CHOOSE the right way," answered the Clock Shop man. "He will."

Chad prayed. Then he smiled. "I know what God wants me to CHOOSE," he said. "God wants me to CHOOSE His way. He would never want me to CHOOSE the wrong way."

Do *you* think God wants you to CHOOSE His way too? Remember, IT IS ALWAYS THE RIGHT TIME TO CHOOSE GOD'S WAY. That's what the Clock Shop man says. That's also what the Bible says.

What the Bible Says
about Choosing God's Way

Here are three important Bible teachings about
CHOOSING GOD'S WAY.

GOD WILL TEACH ME WHAT IS BEST
—*Psalm 25:12*

HELP A CHILD CHOOSE THE RIGHT PATH
—*Proverbs 22:6*

THERE IS A RIGHT TIME FOR EVERYTHING
—*Ecclesiastes 3:1*

Chad's Way to Memorize
a Bible Verse

Chad wants to help you learn at least one good Bible
verse about CHOOSING.

Do you see the Bible teachings about CHOOSING
above? Do you see the Bible verse where each teaching is found? CHOOSE a verse you would like to
memorize. Now find that verse in the box on page
41. CHOOSE the version you like best.

Before you learn a Bible verse, ask, "What does it
say?" Then ask, "What does it *mean?*" Talk with your
parents or teacher about the verse. You will learn the
verse better if you know what God says in it. You will
remember it better if you know what it means. Now
repeat the verse until you memorize it.

Some good things to CHOOSE:

What Jesus
would do.

What your
parents
think is best
for you.

Things that will help you, not hurt you.

PSALM 25:12

What man is he that feareth the Lord? Him shall he teach in the way that he shall choose. *(KJV)*

Who is the man that fears the Lord? Him shall He teach in the way He chooses. *(NKJV)*

Where is the man who fears the Lord? God will teach him how to choose the best. *(TLB)*

Who, then, is the man that fears the Lord? He will instruct him in the way chosen for him. *(NIV)*

PROVERBS 22:6

Train up a child in the way he should go: and when he is old, he will not depart from it. *(KJV)*

Train up a child in the way he should go, and when he is old he will not depart from it. *(NKJV)*

Teach a child to choose the right path, and when he is older he will remain upon it. *(TLB)*

Train a child in the way he should go, and when he is old he will not turn from it. *(NIV)*

ECCLESIASTES 3:1

To every thing there is a season, and a time to every purpose under the heaven. *(KJV)*

To everything there is a season, a time for every purpose under heaven. *(NKJV)*

There is a right time for everything. *(TLB)*

There is a time for everything, and a season for every activity under heaven. *(NIV)*

ECCLESIASTES 9:10

Whatsoever thy hand findeth to do, do it with thy might. *(KJV)*

Whatever your hand finds to do, do it with your might. *(NKJV)*

Whatever you do, do well. *(TLB)*

Whatever your hand finds to do, do it with all your might. *(NIV)*

GALATIANS 6:4

But let every man prove his own work, and then shall he have rejoicing in himself alone, and not in another. *(KJV)*

But let each one examine his own work, and then he will have rejoicing in himself alone, and not in another. *(NKJV)*

Let everyone be sure that he is doing his very best, for then he will have the personal satisfaction of work well done, and won't need to compare himself with someone else. *(TLB)*

Each one should test his own actions. Then he can take pride in himself, without comparing himself to somebody else. *(NIV)*

COLOSSIANS 3:23

And whatsoever ye do, do it heartily, as to the Lord. *(KJV)*

And whatever you do, do it heartily, as to the Lord. *(NKJV)*

Work hard and cheerfully at all you do, just as though you were working for the Lord. *(TLB)*

Whatever you do, work at it with all your heart, as working for the Lord. *(NIV)*

Dawn was not a good
helper. She did not
DO things to help.

    While Mother was busy getting **d**inner, **D**awn sat
in a big chair, reading.
    While Mother was washing **d**ishes, **D**awn still sat
in a big chair, reading.

One **day Dawn** said to Mother, "My friends sometimes call me **Dawn Do-Little.** Why do you think they do that?" So Mother told **Dawn** this story:

Dawn Do-Little and Mother Do-Much

Once there was a little girl named **Dawn**. Some of **Dawn's** friends called her **Dawn Do-Little**. That's because **Dawn** tried to **DO** as little as possible. You might say **Dawn** was lazy.

When it was time to set the table, **Dawn** would **DO** little to help Mother. When it was time to wash dishes, **Dawn** would **DO** little to help Mother.

Dawn Do-Little's Mother was sometimes called Mother Do-Much. Mother did too much while Dawn did too little. If Dawn would DO more, Mother could DO less.

One **day** Mother **Do**-Much got sick. She was too sick to cook **dinner**. When it was time to cook **dinner**, Mother **Do**-Much had to stay in bed. Of course there were no dirty **dishes** to wash. But there was no **dinner** to eat either.

Dawn Do-Little sat in her chair reading. She was waiting for someone to get **dinner** for her.

But there was no one to get **dinner**, because Mother **Do**-Much was too sick. So there *was* no **dinner**.

47

At last **Dawn Do-Little** became hungry. So she asked her mother when they would eat. Then Mother told **Dawn Do-Little** that **Dawn** would eat when someone cooked **dinner** for her. "And who will DO that while I'm sick?" Mother asked.

Suddenly **Dawn** knew who would have to DO it.

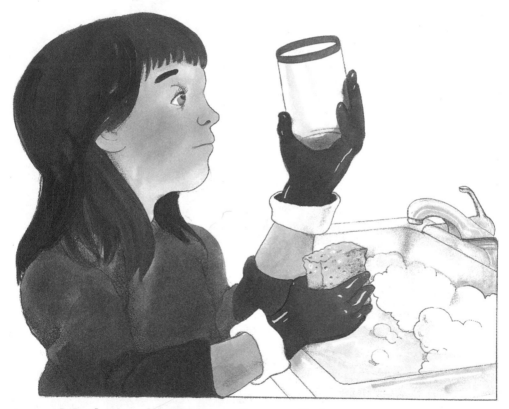

Mother told **Dawn** what to DO. **Dawn** worked hard at getting **dinner**. Then she had to wash and dry her **dishes**. There was no one to help her.

"That was a lot of work," **D**awn told Mother when the **d**ishes were done. "I needed a helper to help me **DO** all that work."

Mother smiled.

"Now I know how much work you **DO**," said Dawn. "From now on, I will be *your* helper. I will help you **DO** the good things you **DO** for us. Then you will have more time to **DO** some things you want to **DO**."

Dawn was never Dawn Do-Little again. She was always **Dawn Do-Much**. So Mother **Do-Much** and Dawn **Do-Much** did much for each other. They also put this special Bible teaching on the refrigerator— DO YOUR BEST.

What the Bible Says
about Doing

Here are three important Bible teachings about DOING.

DO YOUR BEST
—Ecclesiastes 9:10

YOU WILL BE GLAD WHEN YOU DO YOUR BEST
—Galatians 6:4

WHEN YOU DO ANY WORK, DO IT FOR THE LORD
—Colossians 3:23

Dawn's Way to Memorize
a Bible Verse

Dawn wants to help you learn at least one good Bible verse about DOING.

Do you see the Bible teachings about DOING above? Do you see the Bible verse where each teaching is found? Choose a verse you would like to memorize. Now find that verse in the box on page 42. Choose the version you like best.

Team up with someone, like your mother or father or a friend. One person reads the verse. The other reads the reference. Then the other person reads the verse. The first person reads the reference. Keep DOING this until you have learned the verse and the reference.

Which kinds of work should you help your mother or father DO?

E

Eric has some friends. He wants his friends to do what he does, but usually they don't want to do what he does.

Eric wants his friends to follow him, but usually they go the other way.

He wants them to be just like him, and dress like him, and play what he plays. But they don't do any of these things.

One day Eric asked Emily about his friends. "Why don't they do what I do?" he asked. "Why don't they want to be like me and go where I want to go?"

Then Emily told Eric this story:

Eric's Example

Once there was a boy named Eric. He wanted people to do what he did. He wanted them to be like him. He thought they should follow him. But no one would do these things. So Eric felt lonely. He thought no one wanted to play with him.

"Will you play with me?" Eric asked his friend Emily.

"What do you want to play?" Emily asked.

"I want to play **e**lephant," said Eric. "Let me show you. It's exciting. Do exactly what I do."

Eric took a garden hose. When a friend came by, Eric sprayed his friend with water from the hose.

"Wasn't that fun?" Eric asked Emily. "I sprayed water just like an elephant. Now *you* do it."

"No, that was *not* fun," said Emily. "I will not do what you did. What you did was a BAD EXAMPLE of the way you should treat a friend. I do not want to play elephant."

"Oh, I know what we can do," said Eric. "You
will like this. I will be a GOOD EXAMPLE."

Eric sat down on a wooden bench. He sat quietly
for a long time. "What are you doing?" Emily asked.

"I'm being good," said Eric. "I'm staying away
from bad things. Would you like to sit here and be
good too?"

"Doing nothing is OK," said Emily. "But if you
want to be a GOOD EXAMPLE, you should DO
something GOOD."

Then Eric had a great idea. "Will you go to
Sunday School with me on Sunday morning?" he
asked.

"Yes," said Emily. "I will."

Do you think Eric is being a GOOD EXAMPLE now? Would you like to be a GOOD EXAMPLE too?

What the Bible Says
about Being a Good Example

Here are some important Bible teachings about being a GOOD EXAMPLE.

DO WHAT JESUS WOULD DO
—1 Corinthians 11:1

SET A GOOD EXAMPLE BY WHAT YOU SAY AND DO
—1 Timothy 4:12

SET A GOOD EXAMPLE BY DOING GOOD
—Titus 2:7

Eric's Way to Memorize
a Bible Verse

Eric wants to help Emily and you learn at least one good Bible verse about being a GOOD EXAMPLE.

Do you see the Bible teachings about being a GOOD EXAMPLE above? Do you see the Bible verse where each teaching is found? Choose a verse you would like to memorize. Now find that verse in the box on page 63. Choose the version you like best.

Write this verse on at least five cards. Put these cards in places where you will see them often. You may want one on the door of your room. You may want one on the refrigerator door. And you may want one on your favorite toy. Each time you see the card with the verse, read it. Before long, you will memorize it.

Which of these is a GOOD EXAMPLE? Which is a BAD EXAMPLE?

1 CORINTHIANS 11:1

Be ye followers of me, even as I also am of Christ. *(KJV)*

Imitate me, just as I also imitate Christ. *(NKJV)*

And you should follow my example, just as I follow Christ's. *(TLB)*

Follow my example, as I follow the example of Christ. *(NIV)*

1 TIMOTHY 4:12

Be thou an example of the believers, in word, in conversation, in charity, in spirit, in faith, in purity. *(KJV)*

Be an example to the believers in word, in conduct, in love, in spirit, in faith, in purity. *(NKJV)*

Be their ideal; let them follow the way you teach and live; be a pattern for them in your love, your faith, and your clean thoughts. *(TLB)*

Set an example for the believers in speech, in life, in love, in faith and in purity. *(NIV)*

TITUS 2:7

In all things shewing thyself a pattern of good works. *(KJV)*

In all things showing yourself to be a pattern of good works. *(NKJV)*

You yourself must be an example to them of good deeds of every kind. *(TLB)*

In everything set them an example by doing what is good. *(NIV)*

BIBLE VERSES ABOUT FORGIVING

PSALM 86:5

For thou, Lord, art good, and ready to forgive. *(KJV)*

For You, Lord, are good, and ready to forgive. *(NKJV)*

O Lord, you are so good and kind, so ready to forgive. *(TLB)*

You are forgiving and good, O Lord. *(NIV)*

EPHESIANS 4:32

Be ye kind one to another, tenderhearted, forgiving one another, even as God for Christ's sake hath forgiven you. *(KJV)*

Be kind to one another, tenderhearted, forgiving one another, just as God in Christ also forgave you. *(NKJV)*

Be kind to each other, tenderhearted, forgiving one another, just as God has forgiven you because you belong to Christ. *(TLB)*

Be kind and compassionate to one another, forgiving each other, just as in Christ God forgave you. *(NIV)*

F

Fritz likes to play with his friends.
Sometimes he plays football
with them.

Sometimes he
and his friends
play with
fire engines.

Sometimes
they just have
fun together.

Frank sometimes plays with Fritz. One day Frank and Fred were playing with Fritz's favorite fire engine. But when Frank walked across the floor of Fritz's room, he accidentally kicked Fritz's fire engine. Fritz's fire engine was broken.

This made Fritz angry. He told Frank to go home. He told Frank never to come back to his house to play.

Frank was sad. "I'm really sorry, Fritz," Frank said. "Please FORGIVE me." But Fritz would not FORGIVE him.

When Fred saw this, he told Fritz this story:

Frank's Football and Fritz's Fire Engine

One day Fritz went to Frank's house to play football.
Frank was always glad to have Fritz come to play
with him. Frank and Fritz were friends.

Fritz wasn't as careful as he should be. He threw the football over Frank's head. It bounced into the street. Before Fritz and Frank could get it, a big truck went by. The truck ran over the football. The football burst.

Frank was angry. He loved
to play with his football.
Now it was broken.
"Go home!" he said to Fritz.
"I never want to play with
you again."

Fritz was sad. He had caused Frank's special ball to burst. Now he couldn't play with Frank. "I'm sorry, Frank," said Fritz. "Please FORGIVE me." But Frank would not FORGIVE him. Fritz walked sadly away.

Then Fritz sat down on a big log. He was sad. He had caused Frank's football to break. But he was even more sad because Frank would not FORGIVE him.

Suddenly Fritz felt a hand on his shoulder. He looked up. It was Frank. "I FORGIVE you for hurting my football, Fritz," said Frank. "Now please FORGIVE me for hurting *you*." So Fritz and Frank FORGAVE each other. Then they had lots of fun playing together.

When Fritz heard this story from Fred he knew what he had to do. He ran down the street as fast as he could go. Then he saw Frank sitting sadly on a park bench.

Fritz put his hand on Frank's shoulder. Then Frank looked up. "I FORGIVE you for hurting my fire engine, Frank," said Fritz. "Now please FORGIVE me for hurting *you*." Frank and Fritz FORGAVE each other. Then they had lots of fun playing together.

72

What the Bible Says about Forgiving

Here are some important Bible teachings about FORGIVING.

> **GOD WANTS TO FORGIVE US**
> *—Psalm 86:5*

> **WE SHOULD FORGIVE EACH OTHER**
> *—Ephesians 4:32*

Fritz's Way to Memorize a Bible Verse

Fritz wants to help Frank and you learn at least one good Bible verse about FORGIVING.

Do you see the Bible teachings about FORGIVING above? Do you see the Bible verse where each teaching is found? Choose a verse you would like to memorize. Now find that verse in the box on page 64. Choose the version you like best.

Put the Bible verse you have chosen on a card. Use this card as a bookmark in a book you are reading. Every time you open the book and see the bookmark, read the Bible verse. Before long, you will memorize the verse.

Why should you FORGIVE someone? Which of these are true?

Jesus FORGAVE you.

FORGIVING helps friends be friendly again.

FORGIVING others helps to make you happier.

Jesus is pleased when you FORGIVE others.

G

Grace liked to get good **GIFTS**. When **Grace** had a birthday, she often got good birthday **GIFTS**. When it was Christmas, **Grace** got good Christmas **GIFTS**.

Someone gave **Grace** a **g**uitar.
Someone else gave **Grace** a **g**oldfish.
And someone gave **Grace** a pretty **g**lass **g**adget.

Grace liked to get GIFTS. But Grace did not like to GIVE GIFTS. So Grace did not often GIVE anyone a GIFT. If she did, it was not a good GIFT. Grace's grandma was sorry to see this. One day Grace's grandma told Grace this story about GIVING:

Grace the Getter or Grace the Giver?

Once there was a little girl named Grace. People loved her. So they gave her good GIFTS.

Grace loved other people. But she did not GIVE them good GIFTS. She often did not GIVE *any* GIFTS. That's because Grace was a GETTER. She was not a GIVER.

77

One day Ginger asked Grace to play at her house. Grace wanted to play with dolls. But Ginger had no dolls. Ginger also had no TV or stereo or doll house or bike or toy dishes or stuffed animals. Grace saw that Ginger had almost no toys. All Ginger had was a rag doll.

"Why don't you have more toys?" Grace asked Ginger. "Because my parents do not have much money," said Ginger. "My father and mother have not had a job for a long time."

Grace looked around. Ginger and her family did not have many of the good things that Grace's family had.

That night, **Grace** started to play with all her GIFTS. She had many beautiful things. But Grace was not happy. She kept thinking about Ginger. Then Grace talked with her grandma about Ginger.

"Tomorrow, after school, I want to GIVE one of my best dolls to Ginger," she said.

So there were *two* happy girls the next day. Ginger was so happy to have a new doll. And Grace was happy that she was now a GIVER.

When her grandma finished the story, Grace jumped off her lap. "Grandma," she said, "I really do have a friend named Ginger. And she really *doesn't* have any nice things. And I really *do* want to share one of my best dolls with her. May I?"

Grandma smiled. "That would be wonderful," she said. "Grace the GETTER has become Grace the GIVER."

Grandma thought that Grace the GIVER would be much happier than Grace the GETTER. Do you think so?

What the Bible Says about Giving

Here are some Bible teachings about being a GIVER.

GIVE GENEROUSLY
—*Deuteronomy 16:17*

GIVE PART OF ALL YOU GET
—*1 Corinthians 16:2*

GIVE CHEERFULLY
—*2 Corinthians 9:7*

Grace's Way to Memorize a Bible Verse

Grace wants to help you and Ginger learn at least one good Bible verse about GIVING.

Do you see the Bible teachings about GIVING? Do you see the Bible verse where each teaching is found? Choose a verse you would like to memorize. Now find that verse in the box on page 85. Choose the version you like best.

Write each of your favorite memory verses about GIVING on a card. Put each card in an envelope and wrap it like a GIFT. Each day this week, open one of your GIFTS and memorize it. This verse will be a special GIFT to you, and to all you share it with! Do you think your parents might like to help you do this?

Which of these GIFTS could *you* GIVE?

DEUTERONOMY 16:17

Every man shall give as he is able, according to the blessing of the Lord thy God which he hath given thee. *(KJV)*

Every man shall give as he is able, according to the blessing of the Lord your God which he has given you. *(NKJV)*

Give as you are able, according as the Lord has blessed you. *(TLB)*

Each of you must bring a gift in proportion to the way the Lord your God has blessed you. *(NIV)*

1 CORINTHIANS 16:2

Let every one of you lay by him in store, as God hath prospered him. *(KJV)*

Let each of you lay something aside, storing up as he may prosper. *(NKJV)*

Each of you should put aside something from what you have earned during the week. *(TLB)*

Each one of you should set aside a sum of money in keeping with his income. *(NIV)*

2 CORINTHIANS 9:7

God loveth a cheerful giver. *(KJV)*

God loves a cheerful giver. *(NKJV)*

Cheerful givers are the ones God prizes. *(TLB)*

God loves a cheerful giver. *(NIV)*

PSALM 118:13

The Lord helped me. *(KJV)*

The Lord helped me. *(NKJV)*

The Lord helped me. *(TLB)*

The Lord helped me. *(NIV)*

ISAIAH 41:6

They helped every one his neighbor. *(KJV)*

Everyone helped his neighbor. *(NKJV)*

Each man encourages his neighbor. *(TLB)*

Each one helps the other. *(NIV)*

GALATIANS 2:10

We should remember the poor. *(KJV)*

We should remember the poor. *(NKJV)*

We must always remember the poor. *(TLB)*

We should continue to remember the poor. *(NIV)*

H

Heidi wanted a **h**amster for **h**er birthday. Heidi begged for a **h**amster. She even cried a few tears. So Mother bought Heidi a **h**amster for **h**er birthday. But Heidi had not thought about what **h**amsters need.

Heidi's **h**amster needs water.

Heidi's **h**amster needs food.

Heidi's **h**amster needs a clean **h**ome.

"I thought this was Heidi's **h**amster," said
Mother. "If this is Heidi's **h**amster, Heidi must HELP
care for it."

"But I play with my **h**amster," said Heidi.
"And I play with Heidi," said Mother, "But I also
HELP to care for Heidi."
So Mother told Heidi this story about HELPING:

How Heidi Became a Helper

Once there was a girl named **H**eidi. She had a
mother who liked to play with **h**er. Mother and
Heidi often went to the park. Mother HELPED Heidi
swing.

At **h**ome, Mother played with **H**eidi. They dressed dolls and played games. **H**eidi and Mother had lots of fun together.

90

But Mother did not like to
HELP Heidi with her clothes.
When Heidi's clothes were
dirty, Mother did not wash
them. So Heidi had piles of
dirty clothes.

Mother also did not like to HELP Heidi with her food. So Heidi had corn flakes for breakfast. She had oat flakes for lunch. And she had bran flakes for dinner. Soon Heidi had piles and piles of empty cereal boxes.

"Stop! Stop!" said the real Heidi. "You *do* HELP me with my clothes. They never pile up like that. And you get wonderful meals for me. I don't have to eat all that cereal."

"So am I Heidi's HELPER?" asked Mother.

"Yes, you are my wonderful HELPER," said Heidi. Then Heidi hugged her mother. "And I want to be *your* wonderful HELPER. I want to be my hamster's HELPER, too."

So Heidi became a good HELPER. Each day she gave **her h**amster water. She gave **her h**amster food. And she HELPED **her h**amster have a clean **h**ome.

That's how Heidi became a good HELPER. How can *you* become a good HELPER?

What the Bible Says
about Helping

Here are three important Bible teachings about
HELPING.

> **THE LORD HELPS US**
> —Psalm 118:13

> **WE SHOULD HELP EACH OTHER**
> —Isaiah 41:6

> **WE SHOULD HELP THOSE WHO NEED US**
> —Galatians 2:10

Heidi's Way to Memorize
a Bible Verse

Heidi wants to HELP you learn at least one good
Bible verse about HELPING.

Do you see the Bible teachings about HELPING
above? Choose a verse you would like to memorize.
Now find that verse in the box on page 86. Choose
the version you like best.

Write the Bible verse you want to learn on a
card. Read it each morning. When you do, ask,
"Who can I HELP today?" Think of the fun you will
have HELPING others while you learn the verse!

Who is being a good HELPER?

I

Irwin had a problem. Every time he talked with a friend, he talked about himself. He always talked about what "**I**" do. Or he always talked about what "**I**" like.

"I went here and I went there," Irwin said to one friend.

"I did this and I did that," Irwin said to another friend.

"I am bigger than him and better than her," Irwin said to still another friend.

Irene liked Irwin, but she did not like Irwin's "I" problem. So Irene told Irwin this story:

Ira's Ice Cream Shop

One day Ira set up an ice cream stand. It was near the sidewalk in front of his house. He called it Ira's Ice Cream Shop.

"Come and buy," Ira shouted. It was a hot summer day, so some of his friends came with their money to buy ice cream cones.

But **Ira** did not talk about his ice cream. He talked about himself. "I made this stand all by myself," he bragged. "I brought this ice cream here all by myself."

But **Ira's** friends had come to buy ice cream. They did not want to hear about Ira.

By this time, one of Ira's friends had left. Three others stayed. They really wanted to buy some ice cream from Ira. But Ira kept talking, saying "I did this" and "I did that." Soon, another of Ira's friends left. But two stayed to buy ice cream.

"Do you have chocolate?" one friend asked.

"I like vanilla best," said Ira. "I always buy vanilla when I eat ice cream." Ira did not seem to care what his friend wanted. He only cared about what *he* wanted.

So the rest of his friends left. Ira was all alone with his ice cream. No one wanted to buy from him. He did not really want to sell ice cream. He only wanted to talk about himself. Ira had a BIG-I and little-u problem.

Irwin was angry when he heard Irene's story.
"I'd like to tell that Ira kid what I think!" he said.

"What *do* you think?" Irene asked Irwin.

"I think Ira brags too much," said Irwin. "I think
he talks too much about himself and says 'I' too
much."

"That Ira kid is really *you*," said Irene. "You are the boy in the story. And if you don't stop your BIG-I problem, none of your friends will be your friends anymore."

Irwin thought a long time about that. If he didn't like what "that Ira kid" did, he shouldn't like what *he* did. He shouldn't like a BIG-I problem in him any more than he liked it in Ira.

"Please help me stop my BIG-I and little-u problem," he asked Irene. "Help me make it BIG-U and little-I instead."

So Irene became a real friend and helped Irwin change BIG-I to little-I and little-u to BIG-U. That's what a friend *should* do, isn't it?

What the Bible Says
about I and You

Here are three important Bible teachings about PRIDE, which is another name for the BIG-I and little-u problem.

HATE PRIDE BECAUSE GOD HATES PRIDE
—*Proverbs 8:13*

PRIDE CAUSES QUARRELS
—*Proverbs 13:10*

PRIDE CAUSES A PERSON TO FALL
—*Proverbs 16:18*

Irwin's Way to Memorize
a Bible Verse

Irwin wants to help you learn at least one good Bible verse about PRIDE.

Do you see the Bible teachings about PRIDE? Do you see the Bible verse where each teaching is found? Choose a verse you would like to memorize. Now find that verse in the box on page 107. Choose the version you like best.

Write your favorite verse on a card. Put that card on your favorite game or toy. Each time you want to play with that game or toy, read the card three times. Soon you will memorize this verse.

Which of these has a BIG-I and little-u problem?

PROVERBS 8:13

Pride, and arrogancy, and the evil way, and the froward mouth, do I hate. *(KJV)*

Pride and arrogance and the evil way and the perverse mouth I hate. *(NKJV)*

For wisdom hates pride, arrogance, corruption and deceit of every kind. *(TLB)*

I hate pride and arrogance, evil behavior and perverse speech. *(NIV)*

PROVERBS 13:10

Only by pride cometh contention. *(KJV)*

By pride comes only contention. *(NKJV)*

Pride leads to arguments. *(TLB)*

Pride only breeds quarrels. *(NIV)*

PROVERBS 16:18

Pride goeth before destruction, and an haughty spirit before a fall. *(KJV)*

Pride goes before destruction, And a haughty spirit before a fall. *(NKJV)*

Pride goes before destruction and haughtiness before a fall. *(TLB)*

Pride goes before destruction, a haughty spirit before a fall. *(NIV)*

PSALM 35:9

My soul shall be joyful in the Lord. *(KJV)*

My soul shall be joyful in the Lord. *(NKJV)*

I will rejoice in the Lord. *(TLB)*

My soul will rejoice in the Lord. *(NIV)*

PSALM 100:2

Serve the Lord with gladness. *(KJV)*

Serve the Lord with gladness. *(NKJV)*

Obey him gladly; come before him, singing with joy. *(TLB)*

Worship the Lord with gladness. *(NIV)*

JEREMIAH 15:16

Thy word was unto me the joy and rejoicing of mine heart. *(KJV)*

Your word was to me the joy and rejoicing of my heart. *(NKJV)*

Your words bring joy to my sorrowing heart and delight me. *(TLB)*

Your words...were my joy and my heart's delight. *(NIV)*

Jennifer Joy is not always JOYFUL. Sometimes Jennifer is even sad or unhappy.

She is often not JOYFUL when a friend teases her, when she doesn't get what she wants, or when children won't play with the toy she wants them to play with.

"Why are you yelling at me?" Jennifer's little brother asked. "I'm playing with the toy I like. You're playing with the toy *you* like. So why aren't you JOYFUL?"

Jennifer didn't know what to say. So she lay down under a tree in the back yard to think about it. Soon she fell asleep. Then Jennifer had this dream:

Jennifer's Joy Jars

Jennifer dreamed she was walking near a strange town. "Why aren't you JOYFUL?" Jennifer kept asking herself. But she didn't know how to answer this question.

Then Jennifer came to a little shop with a sign in the window that read, "Joy Jars for Sale."

"Perhaps this man will know why I'm not JOYFUL," Jennifer thought. So she asked him.

The man in the shop smiled. "Of course I know," he said. "You need some Joy Jars."

Jennifer was surprised. She had never heard of Joy Jars before. Perhaps you have never heard of Joy Jars either.

"But what do I do with Joy Jars?" Jennifer asked.

"Glad you asked," said the Joy Jar Shop man. "You open them, of course!" So Jennifer took one Joy Jar and opened it. There was nothing but a little card in it. Jennifer took it out.

"It's something from the Joy Book," said the man.

"What's the Joy Book?" Jennifer asked.

"Why, don't you know?" asked the man, surprised. "It's the Bible! When you want only what Jennifer wants, you will be sad. But when you want what God wants, you will be JOYFUL. Each jar has a verse from the Bible. God tells you in each verse something that will make you JOYFUL."

"So that's what will make me JOYFUL," she said. "May I open all three Joy Jars?" When Jennifer did that, she memorized three special Bible verses that helped her know how to be JOYFUL.

When Jennifer woke up, she remembered the Joy Jars. So Jennifer asked Mother to help her make three Joy Jars with special Bible verses about Joy. And Mother was JOYFUL when Jennifer asked to do this!

What the Bible Says about Joy

Here are three important Bible teachings about JOY.

YOU WILL FIND JOY WHEN GOD IS WITH YOU
 —Psalm 35:9

HELPING GOD WILL GIVE YOU JOY
 —Psalm 100:2

READING THE BIBLE WILL GIVE YOU JOY
 —Jeremiah 15:16

Jennifer's Way to Memorize a Bible Verse

Jennifer wants to help you learn at least one good Bible verse about JOY.

Do you see the Bible teachings about JOY above? Do you see the Bible verse where each teaching is found? Choose a verse you would like to memorize. Now find that verse in the box on page 108. Choose the version you like best.

Write the Bible verse you want to learn on a card. Put it in a Joy Jar. Perhaps your mother will help you find some jars you can use.

Do this with your three favorite verses about JOY. Each time you are ready to eat a meal, open a Joy Jar and read how to have JOY. Before long, you will have memorized these favorite verses.

Which way can you show your JOY?

K

King Kirby often did things that were not KIND.
"Why can't he be KIND King Kirby?" some
people asked. "If he was a KIND king, he would not
yell at us, take things from us, and hurt us."

The **king** did not have many friends. Knight Keith was almost his only friend. The **king** listened to him. That's because **Knight Keith** was wise and KIND. **Knight Keith** wanted the king to be KIND, too.

But was he wise enough to help the **king** be more KIND? One day Knight Keith had a plan. He went to see the **king**. "May I tell you a story?" asked the **knight**. "Yes," said the king. "I like stories."
So this is the story **Knight Keith** told **King Kirby:**

A Story of Three Knights

Three **knights** in the land are not KIND. Knight One likes to steal sheep. He already has a hundred sheep. But every day **Knight 1** visits a poor neighbor. He takes one of his neighbors' best sheep.

Yesterday, **K**night One took a poor little girl's pet lamb. He said he was going to eat it for dinner. This poor little girl cried all day. **K**night One isn't very **K**IND, is he?

Knight Two yells at his poor neighbors. He yells at poor old men. He yells at poor old ladies. Knight Two isn't very **KIND**, is he?

Yesterday, **Knight Two** yelled at a poor little boy.
The little boy was so afraid that he cried all day.
Knight Two isn't very **KIND**, is he?

Knight Three is a big bully. He is bigger than his neighbors. So **K**night Three likes to punch other people. Sometimes he pounds a poor man on the head. He even punched a poor little boy the other day. **K**night 3 isn't very KIND, is he?

King Kirby was angry when he heard this story. "These **knights** are not KIND at all!" he shouted. "Bring them here! I will take **Knight** 1's sheep from him. I will yell at **Knight** 2. And I will punch **Knight** 3."

"They are here," said **Knight Keith**. "*You* are **Knight 1**, **Knight 2**, and **Knight 3**. You take things from your people. You yell at them. And you punch them. But don't yell at yourself or punch yourself now. Stop doing these things. Do *KIND* things for your people."

So from that day on, **King Kirby** was the KINDEST king of all. He didn't want to be like **Knight** 1, 2 or 3. Do you?

What the Bible Says
about Doing Kind Things

Here are three important Bible teachings about
being KIND.

BEING KIND TO OTHERS HELPS US TOO
—*Proverbs 11:17*

WE HONOR GOD WHEN WE ARE KIND TO THE POOR
—*Proverbs 14:31*

WE SHOULD BE KIND TO OTHERS
—*Ephesians 4:32*

Keith's Way to Memorize
a Bible Verse

Do you see the Bible teachings about being KIND
above? Do you see the Bible verse where each
teaching is found? Choose a verse you would like to
memorize. Now find that verse in the box on page
129. Choose the version you like best.

Read the verse you have chosen several times.
Each time you read it, think of one way you can be
KIND to others. That will help you remember the
verse. It will also help you DO what the verse says.

Two of these boys or girls are being **KIND**. Two are not.
Which *are* being KIND?

PROVERBS 11:17

The merciful man doeth good to his own soul. *(KJV)*

The merciful man does good for his own soul. *(NKJV)*

Your own soul is nourished when you are kind. *(TLB)*

A kind man benefits himself. *(NIV)*

PROVERBS 14:31

He that honoureth (God) hath mercy on the poor. *(KJV)*

He who honors God has mercy on the needy. *(NKJV)*

To help the poor is to honor God. *(TLB)*

Whoever is kind to the needy honors God. *(NIV)*

EPHESIANS 4:32

Be ye kind one to another. *(KJV)*

Be kind to one another. *(NKJV)*

Be kind to each other. *(TLB)*

Be kind and compassionate to one another. *(NIV)*

JEREMIAH 31:3

I have loved thee with an everlasting love. *(KJV)*

I have loved you with an everlasting love. *(NKJV)*

I have loved you with an everlasting love. *(TLB)*

I have loved you with an everlasting love. *(NIV)*

MATTHEW 22:37

Love the Lord thy God with all thy heart. *(KJV)*

Love the Lord your God with all your heart. *(NKJV)*

Love the Lord your God with all your heart. *(TLB)*

Love the Lord your God with all your heart. *(NIV)*

1 JOHN 3:23

Love one another. *(KJV)*

Love one another. *(NKJV)*

Love one another. *(TLB)*

Love one another. *(NIV)*

L

Lisa ran to her room crying. That's because Mother had to punish her. "Please don't eat a cookie just before dinner," Mother had said. Lisa got into the cookie jar and ate some cookies. So Mother punished her.

"You don't LOVE me," Lisa shouted as she ran to her room. "If you LOVED me, you would let me do what I want to do, say what I want to say, and not go to bed until I want to go to bed."

Mother followed Lisa to her room. "I don't let you do these things because I *do* LOVE you," said Mother. "Do you understand?"

"No," said Lisa. "I think you *would* let me do those things if you really LOVED me."

"Okay, Lisa. I will let you do all those things today," said Mother. "But you must write a story about LOVE tonight."

Lisa was *so* happy. This is the story she wrote late that night:

A Story about Love

This morning I told Mother that she didn't LOVE me. That's because she doesn't let me do everything I want. So she told me I could do everything I want today. All I must do is write this story before I go to bed.

It was so much fun this morning. I asked Mother for a cookie. She said, "You don't need to ask me. You're doing everything you want today." So I took the cookie jar down. I ate all the cookies in the jar.

Then I got sick. You know what *yukky* means, don't you? That's how I felt. I don't think I want another cookie for a long, long time.

Maybe Mother *does* LOVE me. She keeps me from eating too much and feeling yukky every day.

Mother smiled when she saw how yukky I felt. I didn't like that, so I yelled at her. I thought Mother would punish me for yelling at her. But she just smiled.

"It's OK today," she said. "You can say anything you want to say."

So I yelled some more. But suddenly I felt yukky in my *heart*. I really didn't want to yell at my wonderful mother. Maybe she really does LOVE me. She keeps me from yelling at her and feeling yukky in my heart every day.

Mother said I could stay up all night. I thought that would be fun. I watched TV until midnight. Mother read her book. Then I started to yawn. Mother smiled. I wanted to yell at her again. But I couldn't.

"I'm going to bed," I said.

"So early?" Mother asked. I wanted to yell at Mother again. But I couldn't say anything mean to her. I knew I couldn't stay up much longer. And I still had to write this story. So I went to my room and am writing this story.

But do you know what? I think Mother really *does* LOVE me. She doesn't let me stay up late and get too tired every night.

I can't wait to see Mother tomorrow morning.
Will she be surprised! I want to tell her that she
really *does* LOVE me. I know that now. And I want to
tell her that I really LOVE her, too. I can't wait until
mornin....

"Zzzzzz," Lisa said as her head dropped to her
chest. She didn't quite finish writing her last word.
She was sound asleep.

What the Bible Says
about Love

Here are three important Bible teachings about
LOVE.

> **GOD LOVES US FOREVER**
> *—Jeremiah 31:3*
>
> **LOVE GOD WITH ALL YOUR HEART**
> *—Matthew 22:37*
>
> **LOVE EACH OTHER**
> *—1 John 3:23*

Lisa's Way to Memorize
a Bible Verse

Here's how you can learn at least one good Bible
verse about LOVE. Do you see the Bible teachings
about LOVE above? Do you see the Bible verse where
each teaching is found? Choose a verse you would
like to memorize. Now find that verse in the box on
page 130. Choose the version you like best.

Read the verse you have chosen until you have
memorized it. Now read the other verses once. As you
do, keep thinking about the verse you memorized.
What does it say? What does it mean? What do the
other verses say? What do *they* mean? How do these
verses help each other say something special?

Which of these people should we LOVE?

"What are you doing, **Marcie**?" **Mark** asked.
"MEMORIZING a Bible verse," said **Marcie**.
"How do you do that?" asked **Mark**.

So **Marcie** told **Mark** three steps she uses to
MEMORIZE a Bible verse: "I choose a verse I want to
learn. I have a book that helps **me**! I write that verse on
a little card. I read that card many times until I have
MEMORIZED the verse."

"But why?" **Mark** asked. "That's a lot of work! Why do you do it?" So **Marcie** told **Mark** this story:

142

A Walk in the Woods

One night my Father and I went for a walk in the woods. We were trying to find an owl we had heard. It was very dark. "I'm so glad you brought that big flashlight," I said to Father.

"So am I," said Father. "Let me show you what it is like without the flashlight. Hold my hand."

I held Father's hand. Then he turned off the big flashlight. It was SO dark.

"We could not see where to go without it!" I said to Father.

"This flashlight is like the Bible verses you MEMORIZE," said Father. I didn't know what Father meant. So I told him so. Father said he would show **me** when we got home.

When we were home,
Father showed **me** his Bible.
He showed **me** a special verse
in his Bible. It tells how the
Bible is like a big flashlight.
That's because it shows us
where to go.

"Would you like to **MEMORIZE** this verse?" Father asked. I said yes, of course I would. So we wrote it down on a card. I read the card until I knew the verse. Now I will say it every time I think about the Bible. I will say it every time I read a Bible story. And I will say it every time I read my Bible.

Mark thought this was a wonderful story. He wanted to learn this special verse in the Bible too. Would you like to learn it? Then keep reading! Marcie will help you.

What the Bible Says about Memorizing God's Word

Here are three Bible teachings about MEMORIZING God's Word.

MEMORIZE GOD'S WORD TO KEEP FROM SINNING
—Psalm 119:11

MEMORIZE GOD'S WORD SO YOU WILL NEVER FORGET IT
—Psalm 119:16

MEMORIZE GOD'S WORD TO KNOW WHERE TO GO
—Psalm 119:105

Marcie's Way to Memorize a Bible Verse

Marcie wants to help you MEMORIZE Psalm 119:105 and other verses.

Do you see the Bible teachings about MEMORIZING God's Word above? Do you see the Bible verse where each teaching is found? Now find one of those verses in the box on page 151. Choose the version you like best.

For Marcie's favorite verse, Psalm 119:105, draw a picture of a flashlight each time you say it. This will help you always think of God's Word like a flashlight. Each time you MEMORIZE another Bible verse, try to think of a picture you could draw. Choose a picture that will help you remember the verse.

Which of these are true?

The Bible is God's Word.

The Bible tells us what God wants.

The Bible tells us about Jesus.

We should read the Bible each day.

PSALM 119:11

Thy word have I hid in mine heart, that I might not sin against thee. *(KJV)*

Your word I have hidden in my heart, that I might not sin against You. *(NKJV)*

I have thought much about your words, and stored them in my heart so that they would hold me back from sin. *(TLB)*

I have hidden your word in my heart that I might not sin against you. *(NIV)*

PSALM 119:16

I will delight myself in thy statutes: I will not forget thy word. *(KJV)*

I will delight myself in Your statutes; I will not forget Your word. *(NKJV)*

I will delight in God's words and not forget them. *(TLB)*

I delight in your decrees; I will not neglect your word. *(NIV)*

PSALM 119:105

Thy word is a lamp unto my feet, and a light unto my path. *(KJV)*

Your word is a lamp to my feet and a light to my path. *(NKJV)*

Your words are a flashlight to light the path ahead of me, and keep me from stumbling. *(TLB)*

Your word is a lamp to my feet and a light for my path. *(NIV)*

PROVERBS 1:10

If sinners entice thee, consent thou not. *(KJV)*

If sinners entice you, do not consent. *(NKJV)*

If young toughs tell you, "Come and join us"—turn your back on them. *(TLB)*

If sinners entice you, do not give in to them. *(NIV)*

EPHESIANS 6:11

Put on the whole armour of God, that ye may be able to stand against the wiles of the devil. *(KJV)*

Put on the whole armor of God, that you may be able to stand against the wiles of the devil. *(NKJV)*

Put on all of God's armor so that you will be able to stand safe against all strategies and tricks of Satan. *(TLB)*

Put on the full armor of God so that you can take your stand against the devil's schemes. *(NIV)*

JAMES 1:15

When lust hath conceived, it bringeth forth sin: and sin, when it is finished, bringeth forth death. *(KJV)*

When desire has conceived, it gives birth to sin; and sin, when it is full-grown, brings forth death. *(NKJV)*

Evil thoughts lead to evil actions and afterwards to the death penalty from God. *(TLB)*

After desire has conceived, it gives birth to sin; and sin, when it is full-grown, gives birth to death. *(NIV)*

N

"Nina, please take this **n**ewspaper to our next door **n**eighbor," said Mother.

"NO," said Nina. Mother did not like to hear Nina say NO. So Mother talked with Nina about it.

"There are NICE NOs," said Mother. "And there are Not-So-Nice NOs."

"But how do I know which are NICE NOs and which are Not-So-Nice NOs?" asked Nina. So Mother told Nina this story:

Nice NOs and Not-So-Nice NOs

Three mice lived in a cozy little hole in an old house. There was a father mouse, a mother mouse, and a Nina mouse. These were not **n**asty mice, so you might say they were **n**ice mice.

Nina was a **n**eat little mouse who did **n**ice things. But like other girl and boy mice, she sometimes said NO at the wrong time.

One day Nina was playing outside the mouse hole. "Come and help me, Nina," Mother Mouse called. "No," said Nina. Of course Nina did not know that Mother Mouse wanted Nina to help them eat some cheese Father Mouse had found. So when Nina came in, the cheese was gone. That was a Not-So-Nice NO, wasn't it?

One other day, **Nina** was playing outside the mouse hole. "Come here quickly!" Father called. "No," said Nina. But she soon knew why Father had said that. She had to run for her life to get inside the mouse hole. The cat almost had her for lunch! That was also a **Not-So-Nice NO**, wasn't it?

But one day Nina was playing with a friend. This friend was sometimes Not-So-Nice. "Let's go over to the **n**eighbor's house while they are gone," this Not-So-Nice friend said. "Let's steal some cheese!"
"NO!" said Nina. "I would NEVER do that!" Now that was a NICE NO, wasn't it?

When the real Nina heard this story, she smiled. "I really want to say NICE NOs," she said. "I never want to say Not-So-Nice NOs."

I'm sure you can think of many ways to say NICE NOs, can't you? And I'm sure you can think of many Not-So-Nice NOs that you will not say. Next time you start to say a Not-So-Nice NO, think of Nina Mouse and the hungry cat. You won't be hurt by a hungry cat, but you *could* get hurt in some other way.

160

What the Bible Says
about Saying No

Here are three important Bible teachings about saying NO.

DON'T LISTEN WHEN FRIENDS TEMPT YOU
—Proverbs 1:10

ASK GOD TO HELP YOU SAY NO
—Ephesians 6:11

SAY NO TO BAD THINGS TO STAY OUT OF TROUBLE
—James 1:15

Nina's Way to Memorize
a Bible Verse

Nina wants to help you learn at least one good Bible verse about saying NO.

Do you see the Bible teachings about saying NO above? Do you see the Bible verse where each teaching is found? Choose a verse you would like to memorize. Now find that verse in the box on page 152. Choose the version you like best.

Before memorizing each verse, try to say what the verse says in your own words. That will help you think about the meaning of the verse. Now memorize it.

Nina is saying NO in each of these pictures. What would you like to say to her as she says NO?

O

Owen did not like to **OBEY** his parents. "Please don't do that," Mother would say. But Owen would do it anyway.

"Please do this," Father would say. But Owen did not do it.

This made Owen's sister Olive angry. She scolded Owen for not **OBEYING**.

"You don't **OBEY** Mother," she said. "And you don't **OBEY** Father. Be careful, Owen! You may even forget to **OBEY** Jesus!"

163

Owen went outside and sat on a big stump to think about that. What would happen if he didn't OBEY Jesus? What would Jesus think? Then **Owen** began to think about this pretend story:

Owen Learns to Obey

In his pretend story, **Owen** was walking down a path. He saw someone coming to meet him. It was Jesus! He looked just like **Owen** thought Jesus should look. But **Owen** was surprised to see Him. **Owen** was even more surprised when Jesus spoke to him.

"Come with Me," said Jesus. "I will show you something wonderful."

But **Owen** didn't **OBEY** Jesus. He did not go with Jesus. Then **Owen** saw Jesus' face. He looked so *sad*. He looked as sad as Mother had looked when **Owen** did not **OBEY** her.

"Come with Me," Jesus said again. "I will show you something wonderful."

But **O**wen didn't **OBEY** Jesus. He did not go with Jesus. Then **O**wen looked at Jesus' face again. He looked even more sad now. He looked as sad as Father had looked when **O**wen did not **OBEY** him.

"Come with Me," Jesus said a third time. "I will show you something wonderful."

Owen almost OBEYED Jesus this time. But he still didn't go with Him. He still didn't OBEY Him. Then Owen looked at Jesus' face. He almost thought he saw a tear in Jesus' eye. Owen had seen tears in Mother's eyes when he did not OBEY her. He sometimes saw a tear in Father's eyes, too, when he did not OBEY him.

168

"Please don't cry," **Owen** said to Jesus. "I'm really very sorry that I didn't **OBEY** You. I will **OBEY** You from now on."

So **Owen** went with Jesus. Do you know what **Owen** saw? In his pretend story, he saw Mother and Father. He saw himself not **OBEYING** them. They both looked sad. They both had tears in their eyes. They looked so sad that **Owen** had tears in his eyes, too.

Owen's pretend story was suddenly over. He looked up and saw Mother and Father standing near the stump, watching him.

"Please don't cry," Owen shouted. "I'm very sorry that I didn't **OBEY** you. I will **OBEY** you from now on."

Then he jumped from the big stump and ran to Mother and Father. He gave each one a big hug. Mother and Father gave Owen a big hug too. And Owen *did* **OBEY** his parents. Well, he **OBEYED** most of the time. But whenever he didn't, he always thought about Jesus having tears in His eyes. Then Owen **OBEYED**. The next time *you* don't **OBEY**, perhaps you will think of Jesus. You may see tears in His eyes, too.

What the Bible Says
about Obeying

Here are three important Bible teachings about OBEYING.

> **OBEY GOD'S WORD**
> —*Luke 11:28*
>
> **OBEY GOD**
> —*Acts 5:29*
>
> **OBEY YOUR PARENTS**
> —*Ephesians 6:1*

Owen's Way to Memorize
a Bible Verse

Owen wants to help you learn at least one Bible verse about **OBEYING**.

Do you see the Bible teachings and Bible verses above? Choose a verse you would like to memorize. Find that verse in the box on page 173. Choose the version you like best.

Would you like to make a *mobile* of Bible verses? After you choose verses to memorize, write each one on a card. Hang a wire coat hanger on the door of your room, or in another place where you will see it often. Hang your memory cards on the coat hanger, using string or some other fastener. Ask your mother or father to help you. The mobile will remind you of the verses you have memorized.

Which of these people should you **O**BEY?

Your mother?

Your father?

Your friends
who don't
love Jesus?

Jesus?

LUKE 11:28

Blessed are they that hear the word of God, and keep it. *(KJV)*

Blessed are those who hear the word of God and keep it. *(NKJV)*

Blessed are all who hear the Word of God and put it into practice. *(TLB)*

Blessed are those who hear the word of God and obey it. *(NIV)*

ACTS 5:29

We ought to obey God. *(KJV)*

We ought to obey God. *(NKJV)*

We must obey God. *(TLB)*

We must obey God. *(NIV)*

EPHESIANS 6:1

Children, obey your parents. *(KJV)*

Children, obey your parents. *(NKJV)*

Children, obey your parents. *(TLB)*

Children, obey your parents. *(NIV)*

PSALM 5:2

Hearken unto the voice of my cry, my King, and my God: for unto thee will I pray. *(KJV)*

Give heed to the voice of my cry, My King and my God, For to You will I pray. *(NKJV)*

O Lord, hear me praying; listen to my plea, O God my King, for I will never pray to anyone but you. *(TLB)*

Listen to my cry for help, my King and my God, for to you I pray. *(NIV)*

JEREMIAH 33:3

Call unto me, and I will answer thee, and shew thee great and mighty things, which thou knowest not. *(KJV)*

Call to Me, and I will answer you, and show you great and mighty things, which you do not know. *(NKJV)*

Ask me and I will tell you some remarkable secrets about what is going to happen. *(TLB)*

Call to me and I will answer you and tell you great and unsearchable things you do not know. *(NIV)*

JAMES 5:13

Is any among you afflicted? Let him pray. *(KJV)*

Is any among you suffering? Let him pray. *(NKJV)*

Is anyone among you suffering? He should keep on praying about it. *(TLB)*

Is any one of you in trouble? He should pray. *(NIV)*

P

Philip was worried about many things. You might call Philip a *worrier*. Philip's friend Paige asked him one day why he worried so much. So Philip told her.

"My father says he might lose his job. And we might have to move. And I might go to a place where I have no friends."

"You need someone to help you with all this," said Paige. "You're worried because you don't have a helper." Philip looked surprised.

"But who can help me with these things?" he asked. So Paige told Philip this story:

Someone Bigger to Help Me

Long ago, in Bible times, there was a war. David's people were called Israelites. They were fighting the Philistines.

The **Philistines** had a giant named Goliath. He was so big that he couldn't stand up in your house. He was mean, too.

"Send someone to fight me!" Goliath shouted.

But no one wanted to fight Goliath. He was too big for them, just like your **problems** are too big for you. So all the Israelite soldiers were afraid and worried, just like *you* are afraid and worried.

"I'll fight that giant!" said David.

"You're just a boy!" said the Israelite king.

"But I have someone bigger than that giant to help me!" said David. "God will help me." God *was* much bigger than Goliath, wasn't He?

You should have seen Goliath. He was *big*. He must have been twice as big as David. He had a big spear. He had a big sword. He had a big shield. David had nothing but a little sling and five little rocks.

"I'll feed you to the birds!" Goliath shouted at him.

"No you won't! God will help me fight you!"
David shouted back.

And David won! Goliath was bigger, but God
helped David. God was bigger than Goliath. God
can also help you with *your* big problems. He is
much bigger than all of them.

"That's a great story," said **Philip**. "But how do I get God to help me? What do I do?"

"That's easy," said **Paige**. "You *ask* Him! **PRAY!** Then He will help you with *your* giants...those big worries."

"I will, I will!" said **Philip**. So **Philip PRAYED** and asked God to help him. Do you think God *did* help him?

What the Bible Says
about Praying

Here are three important Bible teachings about PRAYING.

> **WHEN WE PRAY, WE ARE TALKING WITH GOD**
> —*Psalm 5:2*

> **GOD HEARS AND ANSWERS PRAYER**
> —*Jeremiah 33:3*

> **WHEN YOU HAVE TROUBLE, PRAY**
> —*James 5:13*

Paige and Philip's Way
to Memorize a Bible Verse

Paige and Philip want to help you learn at least one good Bible verse about PRAYING.

Do you see the Bible teachings about PRAYING above? Do you see the Bible verse where each teaching is found? Choose a verse you would like to memorize. Now find that verse in the box on page 174. Choose the version you like best.

Before you memorize each verse about PRAYING, PRAY. Ask God to help you understand it. Ask Him to help you be different as you do what the verse says.

Remember to **PRAY** tonight.
When you do, remember
to thank God for:

Ask God to help you
with your **problems**.

Thank God for:

Ask God to help your
family and friends.

What else would you like to remember to **PRAY** for?

184

"Quit **QUARRELING**, Quinn!" his friend said. "Can't you be quiet some of the time?" **Quinn's** friend did not like it when **Quinn QUARRELED**.

"You **QUARREL** when we play games, you **QUARREL** when we eat lunch, and you **QUARREL** when we walk home from school."

"I'm sorry," said **Quinn**. "I really don't want to QUARREL with you. I want to *quit* QUARRELING. But what can I do?" So **Quinn's** friend told him this story:

Pride and Patience

Once upon a time, in a land far away, there lived a giant. His name was Pride. This proud giant was always starting a **QUARREL**. That's because he was so proud. He thought his friends should always do things *his* way.

"I'm bigger than you are!" Pride said to his friend. "So you should play the game *I* want to play." Pride *was* much bigger. But his friend did not like what Pride said. So Pride and his friend began to **QUARREL**.

Then a little girl named Patience came along.
"Why are you **QUARRELING**?" she asked.

"I want to play the game *I* want," said the giant.

"And I want to play the game *I* want," said his friend.

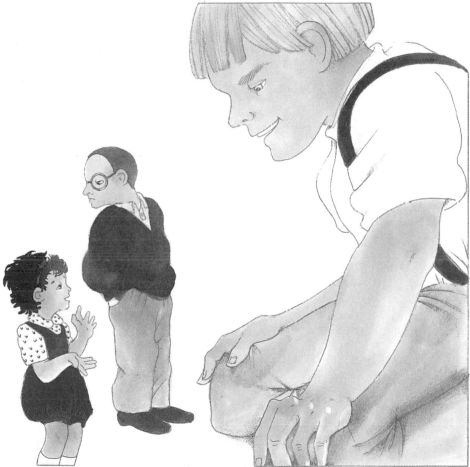

Patience smiled. "Let's sit here quietly until you each want to play the same game," she said. "OK?"

Patience sat with Pride and the man for a long time. At last the giant spoke.

"I've forgotten which game I wanted to play!" he said. "*You* choose."

"Thanks," said his friend. "But you're such a nice friend now, you may choose." Pride and the man almost got into another QUARREL about that. But they didn't.

Before long, Pride and his friend were happily playing their game. No one remembers who chose the game. Patience had stopped the **QUARREL**.

"That was a good story," said **Quinn**. "Pride makes me want *my* way all the time. Patience helps me let others have their way part of the time. Pride causes me to start QUARRELS. Patience keeps me from QUARRELING. Right?"

Quinn's friend smiled. "Right!" he said.

What the Bible Says
about Quarreling

Here are two important Bible teachings about
QUARRELING.

PRIDE CAUSES US TO QUARREL
—Proverbs 13:10

PATIENCE KEEPS US FROM QUARRELING
—Proverbs 15:18

Quinn's Way to Memorize
a Bible Verse

Quinn wants to help you learn at least one good
Bible verse about QUARRELING.

Do you see the Bible teachings about QUARREL-
ING above? Do you see the Bible verse where each
teaching is found? Choose a verse you would like to
memorize. Now find that verse in the box on page
195. Choose the version you like best.

Write your memory verse about QUARRELING
on five cards. Give them to your mother or father.
Ask them to hand one to you the next time you try
to start a QUARREL with someone. Then say your
verse. Do you think that will help you stop your
QUARRELING? Will it help you learn the verse?
Quinn thinks so.

Which of these would start a **QUARREL**? Which would stop a **QUARREL**?

"Which game would you like to play?"

"If you don't let me pitch, I'll take my ball and go home!"

"I'll be glad to come to your house to play."

"If you don't play at my house, I won't play with you."

PROVERBS 13:10

By pride cometh contention. *(KJV)*

By pride cometh only contention. *(NKJV)*

Pride leads to arguments. *(TLB)*

Pride only breeds quarrels. *(NIV)*

PROVERBS 15:18

He that is slow to anger appeaseth strife. *(KJV)*

A wrathful man stirs up strife. *(NKJV)*

A cool-tempered man tries to stop fights. *(TLB)*

A patient man calms a quarrel. *(NIV)*

PSALM 16:9

My heart is glad, and my glory rejoiceth. *(KJV)*

My heart is glad, and my glory rejoices. *(NKJV)*

Heart, body, and soul are filled with joy. *(TLB)*

My heart is glad and my tongue rejoices. *(NIV)*

PSALM 118:24

This is the day which the Lord hath made; we will rejoice and be glad in it. *(KJV)*

This is the day which the Lord has made; We will rejoice and be glad in it. *(NKJV)*

This is the day the Lord has made. We will rejoice and be glad in it. *(TLB)*

This is the day the Lord has made; let us rejoice and be glad in it. *(NIV)*

PHILIPPIANS 4:4

Rejoice in the Lord always. *(KJV)*

Rejoice in the Lord always. *(NKJV)*

Always be full of joy in the Lord. *(TLB)*

Rejoice in the Lord always. *(NIV)*

"Why so grumpy, **Rita**?" a friend asked. "I thought you Christians are supposed to be happy. You were gloomy in class this morning, you were grouchy at lunch time, and you are grumpy now at recess this afternoon."

Rita really *was* sad now. She had been trying to get her friend to come to Sunday School with her.

"I'm sorry," **Rita** said to her friend. "You're right. Christians *should* be happy. I *want* to be."

That night, **Rita** asked her mother what she could do. So her mother told **Rita** a story:

Rita Rejoices

Once there was a girl named **Rita**. She liked to read her Bible and pray. She liked to go to Sunday School. She even asked her friends to go with her to Sunday School. But her friends wouldn't go. Do you know why?

"Why should I go to your Sunday School?" a
friend asked **R**ita. "You're always grumpy or gloomy
or grouchy. Is that what they teach at Sunday
School?"

    Rita knew her friend was right. But what could
she do? Then she had a great idea.

"I will learn a Bible verse about REJOICING today. I'll learn another one tomorrow. And I'll learn still another the next day," said Rita. So Rita found three great Bible verses about REJOICING. She wrote them on little cards. Every time she felt a little grumpy, she read one of these Bible verses. Before long, she knew all three of them.

Soon **Rita** began to **REJOICE**. Each time she said one of her Bible verses, she **REJOICED** even more. The more she **REJOICED**, the more her friends wanted to play with her and be with her. Before long, two friends wanted to go to Sunday School with her.

"That was a wonderful story," the real Rita said
to her mother. "Will you help me choose three good
verses about REJOICING?"

Before long, **Rita** had memorized the three verses about REJOICING that she had chosen. Soon her friends began to play with her more. Two of her friends said they would go to Sunday School with her. Do you think you would like to memorize Rita's three verses about REJOICING? **Rita** will REJOICE if she can share them with you.

What the Bible Says
about Rejoicing

Here are three important Bible teachings about REJOICING.

> **OUR HEARTS AND LIPS SHOULD REJOICE TOGETHER**
> *—Psalm 16:9*
>
> **WE SHOULD REJOICE BECAUSE GOD MADE OUR DAY**
> *—Psalm 118:24*
>
> **WE SHOULD REJOICE IN GOD ALL THE TIME**
> *—Philippians 4:4*

Rita's Way to Memorize
a Bible Verse

Rita wants to help you learn at least one of her Bible verses about REJOICING.

Do you see the Bible teachings about REJOICING above? Do you see the Bible verse where each teaching is found? Choose a verse you would like to memorize. Now find that verse in the box on page 196. Choose the version you like best.

Write each of the verses you wish to memorize on a card. Do you remember what Rita did? Each time she felt grumpy, it reminded her to say one of her verses. It also reminded her to REJOICE, just like the verses say. Do you think these verses will remind *you* to REJOICE too? Rita thinks so.

Which of these should cause us to REJOICE?

When our family loves us?

When our friends are good friends?

When we can read the Bible?

When we know Jesus loves us?

S

Once there were two brothers. These brothers were twins, and they looked exactly alike. But their friends could tell the difference. They knew which brother was Shawn. And they knew which brother was Shane.

"Shane is SELFISH with his things," they said.

"But Shawn SHARES *his* things."

As time went on, friends played more with SHARING Shawn. And they played less with SELFISH Shane. At first, Shane was so SELFISH that he didn't notice he was alone most of the time. Shawn was so busy SHARING that he didn't notice that friends played with him more.

One day, SELFISH Shane noticed that he had no friends. *All* his friends were now playing with SHARING Shawn. When a little girl named Susan saw SELFISH Shane alone, she told this story to Shane:

Susan's Sharing Story

At Sunny Acres, the animals dressed up like people. They talked with each other like people. Some even did SELFISH or SHARING things, just like people.

Stephen Sheep SHARED what he had. But Percival Pig was SELFISH. He wouldn't SHARE anything.

One day Stephen Sheep found a big bag of corn. He was *so* happy. He called all his friends together. They had a wonderful picnic. Then they all played games together. The happiest friend of all was SHARING Stephen Sheep.

On another day, Percival Pig found a big bag of corn. He was also happy. But he took the bag of corn to a lonely corner of the barnyard and ate it all by himself. He thought no one saw him. But all his friends saw him. They thought he was being SELFISH.

Now you know why the animals liked to play games with SHARING Stephen Sheep. And you know why Percival Pig grew more lonely each day, sitting in that all-alone corner of the barnyard.

212

That day a little mouse asked Percival, "Which will make you happier, six ears of corn or six friends?"

"I would rather have six friends than six ears of corn, of course," Percival snorted. But the mouse pretended that he didn't hear Percival. He asked the same question again. Percival gave the same answer.

The mouse asked that same question *six times*. Each time Percival grew more angry. Then suddenly Percival saw what the mouse was saying. SELFISH people get lots of *things*. But they lose lots of *friends*. SHARING people have lots of friends, but they may not have as many things.

"I see it!" SELFISH Shane shouted. "I see it!"

"See what?" Susan asked. "I see what I have been doing! I have been SELFISHLY keeping things while losing friends. I should be keeping *friends* while I SHARE *things*."

So what do you think Shane did next? That's right. He SHARED his toys with his friends. So they all played happily together.

What the Bible Says about
Selfishness and Sharing

Here are some important Bible teachings about SELFISHNESS and SHARING.

SHARE AS GOD HAS SHARED WITH YOU
—Deuteronomy 16:17

FOLLOW GOD, NOT SELFISHNESS
—Psalm 119:36

GOD IS PLEASED WHEN WE SHARE
—Hebrews 13:16

Shawn and Shane's Way to Learn a Bible Verse

Shawn and Shane want to help you learn at least one of these Bible verses about SHARING and SELFISHNESS.

Do you see the Bible teachings above? Do you see the Bible verse where each teaching is found? Choose a verse to memorize. Now find that verse in the box on page 217. Choose the version you like best.

Find a memory partner—a friend or family member. Write the verses about SHARING and SELF-ISHNESS on cards. Each time your memory partner says, "SHARE a Bible verse," you must try to say one of your SHARING verses. If you say it to your partner, he or she must quote it back to you. The object is to "catch" your partner when he or she can't say it.

Which of these should you SHARE?

Your toys?

Your money?

Your talent?

Your help?

DEUTERONOMY 16:17

Every man shall give as he is able, according to the blessing of the Lord thy God which he hath given thee. *(KJV)*

Every man shall give as he is able, according to the blessing of the Lord your God which He has given you. *(NKJV)*

Give as you are able, according as the Lord has blessed you. *(TLB)*

Each of you must bring a gift in proportion to the way the Lord your God has blessed you. *(NIV)*

PSALM 119:36

Incline my heart unto thy testimonies, and not to covetousness. *(KJV)*

Incline my heart to Your testimonies, and not to covetousness. *(NKJV)*

Help me to prefer obedience to making money. *(TLB)*

Turn your heart toward your statutes and not toward selfish gain. *(NIV)*

HEBREWS 13:16

But to do good and to communicate forget not: for with such sacrifices God is well pleased. *(KJV)*

But do not forget to do good and to share, for with such sacrifices God is well pleased. *(NKJV)*

Don't forget to do good and to share what you have with those in need, for such sacrifices are very pleasing to him. *(TLB)*

Do not forget to do good and to share with others, for with such sacrifices God is pleased. *(NIV)*

PSALM 92:1

It is a good thing to give thanks unto the Lord. *(KJV)*

It is good to give thanks to the Lord. *(NKJV)*

It is good to say, "Thank you" to the Lord. *(TLB)*

It is good to praise the Lord. *(NIV)*

COLOSSIANS 3:15

Be ye thankful. *(KJV)*

Be thankful. *(NKJV)*

Always be thankful. *(TLB)*

Be thankful. *(NIV)*

1 THESSALONIANS 5:18

In everything give thanks: for this is the will of God in Christ Jesus concerning you. *(KJV)*

In everything give thanks; for this is the will of God in Christ Jesus for you. *(NKJV)*

Always be thankful, for this is God's will for you who belong to Christ Jesus. *(TLB)*

Give thanks in all circumstances, for this is God's will for you in Christ Jesus. *(NIV)*

T

It was time for Tina's birthday party. She invited three friends and they all came. Each friend brought Tina a birthday gift. After some games and cake, it was time for Tina to open her birthday gifts.

Tammie gave Tina a stuffed teddy bear. But Tina forgot to say THANKS. Terry gave Tina a stuffed panda bear. But Tina forgot to say THANKS. Tiffany gave Tina a stuffed polar bear. But Tina forgot to say THANKS.

Tina's friends didn't like this. They thought Tina should have said THANKS to each of them.

"Haven't you forgotten something?" Tammie asked Tina.

Tina looked under the wrapping paper. She thought she had forgotten to open a gift.

"Haven't you forgotten to *say* something?" Terry asked Tina.

"I think I need a stuffed koala bear next time," said Tina.

"Haven't you forgotten to say THANKS?" Tiffany asked Tina. Then Tiffany told Tina this story:

The Thank You Bears

Teddy Bear had a birthday party. He invited three friends and they all came. Koala Bear brought a gift. Polar Bear brought a gift. And Panda Bear brought a gift.

After cake and ice cream, it was time to open gifts. Teddy opened Koala Bear's gift. It was a little stuffed Tina doll. But he forgot to say THANKS to Koala Bear for the gift. Next, Teddy opened Polar Bear's gift. It was a little stuffed Tammie doll. But Teddy forgot to say THANKS to Polar Bear for the gift.

At last Teddy opened Panda Bear's gift. It was a little stuffed Terry doll. But Teddy forgot to say THANKS to Panda Bear. Teddy's three friends were sorry that Teddy didn't say THANKS.

Koala Bear picked up the Tina doll. He pretended that the Tina doll was talking to Teddy. "Can't you say THANKS for me?" the Tina doll asked. "If you can't, I'll go home!"

Polar Bear picked up the Tammie doll. He pretended that the Tammie doll was talking to Teddy. "Can't you say THANKS for me?" the Tammie doll asked. "If you can't, I'll go home!"

Panda Bear picked up the Terry doll. He pretended that the Terry doll was talking to Teddy. "I think I'll go home too!" she said. "I don't want to be with someone who can't say THANKS."

"I'm very sorry, friends," said Teddy Bear. "That was rude for me to forget to say THANKS. So THANKS to each of you for the wonderful gifts."

"I want to say THANKS to each of you, too," said the real Tina. "THANKS for the wonderful gifts you brought. I really *do* appreciate them."

Next time *you* receive a gift, any gift, you will remember to say THANKS, won't you?

What the Bible Says about
Saying Thanks

Here are some important Bible teachings about
THANKFULNESS.

IT IS GOOD TO GIVE THANKS TO THE LORD
—Psalm 92:1

BE THANKFUL
—Colossians 3:15

GOD WANTS YOU ALWAYS TO BE THANKFUL
—1 Thessalonians 5:18

Tina's Way to Memorize a Bible Verse

Tina is glad she learned to say THANKS. She wants to
help you learn at least one Bible verse about saying
THANKS. These verses can help you remember to say
THANKS to God, your family, and your friends.

Do you see the Bible teachings about saying
THANKS above? Do you see the Bible verse where
each teaching is found? Choose a verse you would
like to memorize. Now find that verse in the box on
page 218. Choose the version you like best.

Write your Bible verses about THANKS on little
cards. Pin each card with a safety pin to one of your
favorite stuffed animals. Each time you want to play
with that stuffed animal, say the verse. Then each
time you put that stuffed animal away, say the verse
again.

When should you give **THANKS** to God? Find the right signs below.

"Ursula, you're the UGLIEST girl in the world!" Ursula was looking at herself in the mirror.

"That's not true!" said a voice behind Ursula. It was her mother. She had heard what Ursula said.

"But I *am* UGLY," said Ursula. "I don't like my hair, I don't like my feet, and I don't like my fingers."

Ursula didn't say she was too big, too little, too tall, too short, too fat, or too skinny. She just thought she was too *UGLY*.

"Good friends come with all kinds of hair, feet, and fingers," said Mother. "Those things don't make a girl beautiful or a boy handsome."

"But what does?" asked Ursula. Then Mother told Ursula this story:

The Most Un-Ugly Girl in the World

Once there was a girl named Ursula who thought she was UGLY. She didn't like her hair. She didn't like her feet. She didn't like her fingers. Actually, she didn't like *most* of her looks. So this girl thought she was UGLY.

This girl Ursula, who thought she was UGLY, was also the most UNSELFISH girl you will ever meet. One day a neighbor lady came to see Ursula's mother. She brought her little girl with her. Ursula shared her toys with this little girl. She played with her. She even gave one of her toys to this little girl to keep.

At last it was time for the neighbor lady to go home. Ursula heard the neighbor lady say to her mother, "Your Ursula is the most beautiful young lady I have ever met. I have never known such an UNSELFISH girl."

"What did the neighbor lady mean?" Ursula asked when the lady had left. "Can't she see my UGLY hair, my UGLY feet, and my UGLY fingers?" Mother smiled.

"She can see your hair, your feet, and your fingers," said Mother. "But they don't look UGLY because you do so many beautiful things with them."

"But don't my feet and fingers and hair make me look UGLY?" asked Ursula.

"No, my little darling," said Mother. "People would still think you are beautiful if you had 12 toes, 15 fingers, and hair that looked like old rope. You have a beautiful, UNSELFISH heart, and that makes you seem beautiful all over."

The real Ursula smiled a big smile and gave her mother a hug when she heard this story. "Oh, Mother, thank you for that wonderful story," she said. Mother smiled back at Ursula.

"*You* are the girl in that story," she said. "You are truly the most beautiful, most UNSELFISH girl I know."

"Even with my fingers and toes and hair?" Ursula asked.

"Even if you had 12 toes, 15 fingers, and hair that looked like old rope," said Mother.

What the Bible Says about Being Ugly or Beautiful

Here are some important Bible teachings about what it means to be truly beautiful.

> **WE ARE BEAUTIFUL IF WE HAVE A GOOD HEART**
> *—1 Samuel 16:7*
>
> **GOD IS A BEAUTIFUL PERSON**
> *—Psalm 27:4*
>
> **GOD MADE A BEAUTIFUL CREATION**
> *—Ecclesiastes 3:11*

Ursula's Way to Memorize a Bible Verse

Ursula was so glad when she learned how God and His people see UGLINESS and BEAUTY. She would like to help you learn at least one Bible verse about what BEAUTY and UGLINESS really are.

Do you see the Bible teachings above? Do you see the Bible verse where each teaching is found? Choose a verse you would like to remember. Now find that verse in the box on page 239. Choose the version you like best.

Write the verses you want to learn on little cards. Tape them on the mirror you use when you brush your teeth. Each time you are tempted to say "I'm UGLY," read or say the verses again. Then thank God that He sees you, and His friends see you, on the *inside*.

Which would you rather have? Would you rather have God say, "You have a beautiful heart," or have a friend say, "You have a beautiful face?"

Would you rather hear someone say, "She's a beautiful person," or "She has beautiful clothes"?

Would you rather have your mirror tell you that you *look* beautiful, or have your parents say that you *are* a beautiful person?

1 SAMUEL 16:7

The Lord seeth not as man seeth; for man looketh on the outward appearance, but the Lord looketh on the heart. *(KJV)*

The Lord does not see as man sees; for man looks at the outward appearance, but the Lord looks at the heart. *(NKJV)*

Men judge by outward appearance, but I look at a man's thoughts and intentions. *(TLB)*

Man looks at the outward appearance, but the Lord looks at the heart. *(NIV)*

PSALM 27:4

Behold the beauty of the Lord. *(KJV)*

Behold the beauty of the Lord. *(NKJV)*

Delighting in his incomparable perfections and glory. *(TLB)*

Gaze upon the beauty of the Lord. *(NIV)*

ECCLESIASTES 3:11

He hath made every thing beautiful in his time. *(KJV)*

He has made everything beautiful in its time. *(NKJV)*

Everything is appropriate in its own time. *(TLB)*

He has made everything beautiful in its time. *(NIV)*

COLOSSIANS 3:15

Let the peace of God rule in your hearts. *(KJV)*

Let the peace of God rule in your hearts. *(NKJV)*

Let the peace of heart which comes from Christ be always present in your hearts and lives. *(TLB)*

Let the peace of Christ rule in your hearts. *(NIV)*

1 THESSALONIANS 5:13

Be at peace among yourselves. *(KJV)*

Be at peace among yourselves. *(NKJV)*

No quarreling among yourselves. *(TLB)*

Live in peace with each other. *(NIV)*

1 TIMOTHY 2:2

That we may lead a quiet and peaceable life in all godliness and honesty. *(KJV)*

That we may lead a quiet and peaceable life in all godliness and reverence. *(NKJV)*

That we can life in peace and quietness, spending our time in godly living and thinking much about the Lord. *(TLB)*

That we may live peaceful and quiet lives in all godliness and holiness. *(NIV)*

Vince was trying to put the uniform on his space man. But it didn't go on the way he thought it should. So Vince threw the space man across the room. Vince's friend Vic did not like to see that.

"I don't want to play with you if you're going to be so VIOLENT," said Vic.

"What's wrong with that?" asked Vince. "That's the way they do it on TV. They shoot people. They beat up on people. And they crash cars. So what's wrong with that?"

"VIOLENT people hurt others," said Vic.
"Sometimes *they* get hurt too. And VIOLENCE
doesn't please parents or Jesus. That's why I don't
like it." Then Vic told Vince this story:

Three Wooden Soldiers

Once there were three wooden soldiers. They lived on a shelf in Vince's room. These were happy wooden soldiers. All they had to do was to march in a wooden soldier parade now and then. That's why happy smiles were painted on their faces.

Every night, **V**ince watched TV. When he did, he brought his wooden soldiers out so he could play with them while he watched. But **V**ince watched a lot of VIOLENT programs. People shot at each other. They banged each other. And they bumped each other's cars.

Vince saw all of this stuff. So did his wooden soldiers.

The wooden soldiers even saw Vince throw his space man across the room. The more VIOLENCE they saw, the more they began to change. One day when Vince was at school, the wooden soldiers got into a fight. They had never fought before. But they did today. They began to throw things at each other. Before long, Vince's toys were scattered all over his room. And, of course, some of them were broken.

When **Vince** came home, he saw what had
happened. He saw his wooden soldiers standing on
his shelf. He could see that their faces were different.
They did not have the happy smiles that had been
painted on them. The soldiers now had angry faces
instead. Vince was angry, too. He wanted to throw
his soldiers across the room. But he knew that
wouldn't clean up the mess. It wouldn't change his
soldiers, either.

"It's all that VIOLENCE I have been watching with them," Vince finally said to himself. "If that's what it's doing to my soldiers, what is it doing to *me?*" he wondered. Then Vince made a decision. He knew those VIOLENT TV programs did not please Jesus. And they were not good for him or his wooden soldiers.

"I will not watch those VIOLENT programs again," Vince said aloud. When he said that, Vince thought he saw smiles on the faces of his wooden soldiers again. He wasn't sure. But it did *seem* like smiles.

"That was a great story," the real Vince said to Vic. "I understand now. That VIOLENCE really *is* changing me. I'm going to stop watching those VIOLENT TV programs too, just like the Vince in the story." Then Vince looked up at the wooden soldiers on his shelf. He was quite sure he saw a smile on their faces. Do you think he did?

What the Bible Says about
Violence and Peacefulness

Here are some important Bible teachings about
VIOLENCE and PEACEFULNESS.

> PEACEFULNESS COMES FROM THE LORD
> —Colossians 3:15
>
> LIVE PEACEFULLY WITH EACH OTHER
> —1 Thessalonians 5:13
>
> A GODLY AND HOLY LIFE IS PEACEFUL AND QUIET
> —1 Timothy 2:2

Vince's Way to Memorize
a Bible Verse

Vince would like to help you memorize some Bible
verses about VIOLENCE and PEACEFULNESS.

Do you see the Bible teachings above? Do you
see the Bible verse where each teaching is found?
Choose at least one verse you would like to remember. Now find that verse in the box on page 240.
Choose the version you like best.

Write the verses you want to learn on little cards.
Tape them near your TV set where you will see them
each time you start to turn it on. Say each verse you
have learned before you let yourself watch any TV.
These verses will help you choose the right programs
and stay away from TV VIOLENCE. See how much
more PEACEFUL your life will become!

Which of these could be hurt when someone is VIOLENT?

The person to whom someone is VIOLENT?

The person who has been VIOLENT?

Family members?

Jesus?

Wendy was wonderful. But Wendy also was a **WORRIER**. When **Wendy** should have been **WORKING**, she was **WORRYING** instead. When Mother asked **Wendy** to do some chores, **Wendy** would **WORRY** instead of **WORK**.

Wendy **WORRIED** that she wouldn't know what to do. She **WORRIED** that she wouldn't do her chores well. And she **WORRIED** that she wouldn't finish on time.

"WORRIERS don't get their WORK done," said Wendy's friend Ward. "There's a better way to get your WORK done than to WORRY about it."

Then Ward told Wendy this story:

The Worry Medicine

Once there was a wonderful girl named Wendy. Her mother asked her to do three chores. They were easy chores. But Wendy couldn't get her WORK done. That's because she WORRIED instead of WORKED.

The first chore was, "Please set the table for me." But Wendy WORRIED that she wouldn't know what to do. So she didn't do anything. Mother had to set the table. Wendy felt sad about that.

The second chore was, "Please help me dry the dishes." But Wendy WORRIED that she would drop some dishes. So she didn't do anything. Mother dried all the dishes. Wendy also felt sad about that.

The third chore was, "Please sweep the floor for me." But **Wendy** **WORRIED** that she wouldn't get done on time. So she didn't even start. Mother swept the floor. **Wendy** was sad about that, too.

"I want to **WORK** instead of **WORRY**," **Wendy** said to Mother. "What can I do?"

"I will fix some
WORRY medicine for
you," said Mother.

Wendy was curious.
"Will it taste bad?" she
asked.

"Oh, no," said
Mother. "This is good
medicine to take. You
will like it."

Wendy watched while Mother taped three little
cards to a bottle. Then Mother set the bottle with the
cards on the kitchen table.

"Is that the **WORRY** medicine?" Wendy asked.

"Yes," said Mother. "Whenever you start to **WORRY**, read one of these little cards. There is a special Bible memory verse on each card. Read it several times until you memorize it. The Bible verse will help you stop **WORRYING**."

"What a wonderful story!" said the real Wendy. "And what a wonderful idea. I will ask Mother to help me make some **WORRY** medicine right now."

Do you think the **WORRY** medicine helped Wendy stop WORRYING? Do you think **WORRY** medicine can help *you* stop WORRYING?

What the Bible Says about Worrying and Working

Here are some important Bible teachings about WORRYING and WORKING.

YOU SHOULD NOT WORRY
—Matthew 6:25

WORRY WILL NOT HELP YOU
—Matthew 6:27

WORK TO PLEASE THE LORD
—Colossians 3:23

Wendy's Way to Memorize a Bible Verse

Do you see the Bible teachings about WORRYING and WORKING above? Do you see the Bible verse where each teaching is found? Choose a verse you would like to remember. Now find that verse in the box on page 261. Choose the version you like best.

Write each verse on a little card. Next, tape the cards on an empty bottle. Put this bottle where you will see it often, like on the kitchen table. Whenever you WORRY about WORKING, read one verse until you memorize it. Even when you have memorized each verse, continue to take your WORRY medicine (reading and memorizing the verses). That will help you remember what the Lord wants you to do.

Which do you think will please Jesus more:

WORRYING about drying dishes, or *helping* your mother dry the dishes?

WORRYING about feeding your pet, or *feeding* your pet when you should?

WORRYING about doing your home-work, or *doing* your homework?

MATTHEW 6:25

Take no thought for your life, what ye shall eat, or what ye shall drink; nor yet for your body, what ye shall put on. *(KJV)*

Do not worry about your life, what you will eat or what you will drink; nor about your body, what you will put on. *(NKJV)*

Don't worry about things—food, drink, and clothes. *(TLB)*

Do not worry about your life, what you will eat or drink; or about your body, what you will wear. *(NIV)*

MATTHEW 6:27

Which of you by taking thought can add one cubit unto his stature? *(KJV)*

Which of you by worrying can add one cubit to his stature? *(NKJV)*

Will all your worries add a single moment to your life? *(TLB)*

Who of you by worrying can add a single hour to his life? *(NIV)*

COLOSSIANS 3:23

Whatsoever ye do, do it heartily, as to the Lord, and not unto men. *(KJV)*

Whatever you do, do it heartily, as to the Lord and not to men. *(NKJV)*

Work hard and cheerfully at all you do, just as though you were working for the Lord and not merely for your masters. *(TLB)*

Whatever you do, work at it with all your heart, as working for the Lord, not for men. *(NIV)*

MATTHEW 28:20

I am with you alway, even unto the end of the world. *(KJV)*

I am with you always, even to the end of the age. *(NKJV)*

I am with you always, even to the end of the world. *(TLB)*

I am with you always, to the very end of the age. *(NIV)*

JOHN 15:9

As the Father hath loved me, so have I loved you. *(KJV)*

As the Father loved Me, I also have loved you. *(NKJV)*

I have loved you even as the Father has loved me. *(TLB)*

As the Father has loved me, so have I loved you. *(NIV)*

JOHN 15:12

This is my commandment, that ye love one another, as I have loved you. *(KJV)*

This is my commandment, that you love one another as I have loved you. *(NKJV)*

I demand that you love each other as much as I love you. *(TLB)*

My command is this: Love each other as I have loved you. *(NIV)*

JOHN 15:14

Ye are my friends, if ye do whatsoever I command you. *(KJV)*

You are my friends if you do whatever I command you. *(NKJV)*

You are my friends if you obey me. *(TLB)*

You are my friends if you do what I command. *(NIV)*

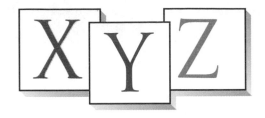

"Mine!" said Yancy. He did not want to share his toys with his friends. Yancy liked words such as "mine," "my," "me," and "I." But Yancey's friends didn't like to play with someone who often said these words.

During playtime, Yancey would often say things like: "Those are MY toys," or "That's MINE," or "I want to do this," or "I want to do that."

"YOU won't have many friends if YOU are always saying words like those," said Yancey's friend Yvonne.

"So what words *should* I say?" asked Yancey.

"YOU might learn to say YOU or YOUR a few times," said Yvonne. Then Yvonne told Yancey this story:

264

Jesus and You

Once there was a boy named Me-Myself-and-I. That's a strange name for a boy. But this boy had a strange problem. All he could say was "Me-Myself-and-I." That's because this boy thought only of himself.

Me-Myself-and-I did not have many friends. It was hard to have a friend who could only say, "Me-Myself-and-I." One day a new boy came to school.

"My name is George," said the new boy. "What is YOUR name?" Of course the boy said, "Me-Myself-and-I." George thought that was strange, but he asked the boy to come to his house to play anyway.

"Who are YOUR best friends?" George asked. "Me-Myself-and-I," said the boy. "But who do YOU share YOUR toys with?" asked George. "Me-Myself-and-I," said the boy. "Would YOU like to play with me?" George asked. "Or would YOU rather play with YOURSELF?" "Me-Myself-and-I," said the boy.

"YOU need to meet my best Friend," said George. "His name is Jesus. He will help YOU learn some other words." Me-Myself-and-I smiled. No one had ever asked him to be Jesus' friend.

"Jesus loves YOU very much," said George. "Me-Myself-and-I?" asked Me-Myself-and-I.

"Yes, YOU!" said George. Then George told his new friend all about Jesus.

"Would YOU like to be Jesus' friend?" asked George. "Would YOU like JESUS AND YOU to be best friends?" The boy nodded his head yes.

Before long this boy was reading his Bible every day. He even memorized some special Bible verses about JESUS AND YOU. Soon he had a new name. And he had new friends, too. That's because Jesus helped him learn to say YOU.

"JESUS AND YOU are best friends," George said to the boy one day. The boy smiled and nodded yes. Do YOU think JESUS AND YOU should become best friends too?

"That's a great story," said Yancey. "I'd like Jesus to be *my* best friend too."

"JESUS AND YOU?" asked Yvonne. Yancey nodded yes.

Now **Yancey** and **Yvonne** want to ask **YOU** if JESUS AND YOU should be best friends. Do **YOU** think so?

What the Bible Says about Jesus and You

Here are some important Bible teachings about JESUS AND YOU.

JESUS WILL BE WITH YOU ALWAYS
—*Matthew 28:20*

JESUS LOVES YOU
—*John 15:9*

JESUS WANTS YOU TO LOVE OTHERS AS HE LOVES YOU
—*John 15:12*

JESUS WANTS YOU TO BE HIS FRIEND
—*John 15:14*

Yancey's Way to Memorize a Bible Verse

Do YOU see the Bible teachings about JESUS AND YOU above? Do YOU see the Bible verse where each teaching is found? Choose a verse YOU would like to remember. Now find that verse in the box on page 262. Choose the version YOU like best.

Print the words JESUS AND YOU on a sheet of paper. Write the memory verses about JESUS AND YOU on little cards. Put these cards on the sheet of paper near the words JESUS AND YOU. Each time you see the words JESUS AND YOU, YOU will remember to say one of these verses. Before long, YOU will have them memorized!

Look at each of these words. Which ones remind you of the word ME? Which ones remind YOU of the word YOU?

Share

MINE

SELFISH

Together

26 Ways to Memorize Bible Verses

1. **READ THE WHOLE VERSE MANY TIMES:** Read the verse several times to yourself. Then read it several times to someone else, like your mother or father. Now try to say the verse to that person without reading it. Keep doing this until you have it memorized.

2. **REPEAT PARTS OF EACH VERSE:** Say several words of a verse several times. Next, say more words of the verse several times. Now say the entire verse several times. Keep doing this until you have memorized the verse. Do you know it? Be sure to learn the reference, too.

3. **UNDERSTAND WHAT THE VERSE SAYS FIRST:** Before you learn a Bible verse ask, "What does it mean?" Talk with your parents or teacher about the verse. You will learn and remember the verse better if you know what it means. Now repeat the verse until you have memorized it.

4. **LEARN AS A TEAM:** Team up with someone, like your mother or father, brother or sister, or a friend. One person reads the verse, then the other person reads the reference. Then switch, so that the other person reads the verse and the first person reads the reference. Keep doing this until you have learned the verse and the reference.

5. **PUT THE VERSE IN FAMILIAR PLACES:** Write the verse on at least 5 cards. Put these cards in places where you will see them often. You may want one on the door of your room. You may want one on the refrigerator door. Does your father or mother take you to school? You may want to keep a card in your car. Each time you see the card with the verse, read it. Before long, you will memorize it.

6. **USE THE BIBLE VERSE AS A BOOKMARK:** Put the Bible verse you have chosen on a card. Use this card as a bookmark in a book you are reading. Every time you open the book and see the bookmark, read the Bible verse. Before long, you will memorize it.

7. **GIVE YOURSELF A BIBLE VERSE GIFT:** Write each verse you want to learn on a card. Put each card in an envelope and wrap it like a special gift. Each day this week open one of your gifts and memorize it. This verse will be a special gift to you, and to all you share it with.

8. **ASK HOW YOU CAN HELP SOMEONE WITH THAT VERSE:** Write the Bible verse you want to learn on a card. Read it each morning. When you do, ask, "Who can I help today? How can this verse help me help that person?" Think of ways you can apply this verse by being a helper. Think of the fun you will have helping while you learn each verse.

9. **REWARD YOURSELF WITH YOUR FAVORITE TOY:** Write your favorite verse on a card. Put that card on your favorite game or toy. Each time you want to play with that game or toy, read the card three times. Before long you will memorize this favorite verse.

10. **FILL SOME MEMORY JARS WITH VERSES:** Write the Bible verses you want to learn on cards. Put them in a Memory Jar, a jar you can keep on your table or desk. Instead of pulling candy or cookies from the Memory Jar, you pull a memory verse each day. Read it until you know it.

11. **THINK OF THREE WAYS YOU CAN DO WHAT YOUR MEMORY VERSE TEACHES:** What does the verse teach? Kindness? Love? Friendliness? Read the verse three times. Each time you read the verse, ask how you can be kind, or loving, or friendly, or whatever the verse

teaches. By the time you memorize it, you will know three ways to do what the verse teaches.

12. **THINK HOW OTHER BIBLE VERSES RELATE TO THIS ONE:** Read the Bible verse you choose until you memorize it. Now read other Bible verses that relate to it (perhaps the same topic, same chapter, same teaching, and so on). Each time you read another Bible verse, think how it relates to the first one you learned. How does each verse help others say something special?

13. **PICTURE THE VERSE YOU LEARN:** What picture do you think of when you say your favorite memory verse? Draw that picture as you think about that verse. Do this each time you memorize a verse. Choose a picture that will help you remember the verse. Example: Draw a heart when you memorize Psalm 119:11, about hiding God's Word in your heart.

14. **SAY THE VERSE FIRST IN YOUR OWN WORDS:** Before you memorize each verse, try to say what the verse says in your own words. That will help you think about the meaning of the verse. Now memorize it.

15. **MAKE A MOBILE OF BIBLE VERSES:** After you choose some verses to memorize, write each one on a card. Hang a wire coat hanger on the door of your room, or somewhere you will see it often. Hang your memory verses on the coat hanger, using string or some other fastener. Ask your mother or father to help you. The mobile will remind you of the verses you have memorized.

16. **TRY TO DO WHAT THE VERSE SAYS BEFORE MEMORIZING IT:** Is the verse about praying? Pray first. It is about being honest? Ask if you have done something dishonest lately. Is it about love? Tell someone you love him or her.

17. **ASK YOUR MOTHER OR FATHER TO GIVE YOU A CARD WHEN YOU DON'T DO WHAT THE VERSE SAYS:** Write some memory verses on cards. Ask Mother or Father to give you a card when you are not doing what the verse says. Then play a game that you must memorize that verse. Example: If the verse is about quarreling, ask your mother or father to hand that card to you if you quarrel with your brother or sister. Then memorize the verse.

18. **MAKE YOUR MIRROR A BIBLE REMINDER:** Write on cards some verses about what you should do. Should you rejoice? Write a verse about rejoicing on a card. Should you share? Write a verse about sharing on a card. Put these cards on the side of your mirror. Each morning, ask if you forgot to do one of these things yesterday. If you did, memorize that verse.

19. **PLAY A PARTNER GAME:** Write verses about a topic on cards. For example, you may choose a topic like sharing. When you least expect it, your partner will say SHARING. Then you must quote a verse on sharing. You will also do this with your partner. The object is to catch your partner when he or she can't say a verse about that topic.

20. **MAKE A BIBLE MEMORY STUFFED ANIMAL ZOO:** Write Bible verses on cards. Pin each card with a safety pin to one of your favorite stuffed animals. Each time you want to play with that stuffed animal, say that verse. Then each time you put that stuffed animal away, say the verse again.

21. **BUILD SOME BIBLE BOOSTERS:** Do you have problems thinking you're not as good as others? You may need some Bible boosters. Write on little cards some Bible verses that say how much God thinks of you. Put these on your mirror. When you look in the

mirror and think you are too ugly, or skinny, or fat, or tall, or something else, memorize one of these verses.

22. **USE EVEN YOUR TV TO HELP YOU MEMORIZE BIBLE VERSES:** Tape some Bible verses near your TV. Don't let yourself turn on the TV until you have memorized a Bible verse.

23. **MAKE A BIBLE MEDICINE BOTTLE:** Tape some memory cards on a bottle you would throw away. Put that Bible medicine bottle on your kitchen table, or near wherever you eat your meals. Read one verse on the bottle at each meal until you memorize it. It will be like good medicine to help you do good things.

24. **FOLLOW A TOPICAL MEMORY PROGRAM:** Do you want to memorize several verses about one topic, such as honesty? Write the word HONESTY with big letters on a sheet of paper. Put little memory cards about this topic around the word. Each time you see the word, read a verse. Before long, you will have the verse memorized.

25. **MAKE A MEMORY PICTURE BOOK:** Staple some sheets of paper together to make a booklet. Write one verse you want to memorize on each sheet. Now find a picture in a magazine that helps you remember that verse. Use this Memory Picture Book to help you memorize these favorite verses. Use the book in a few weeks to review.

26. **PREPARE BIBLE MEMORY BAGS:** Do you take your lunch to school in a paper bag? If so, print your Bible memory verse on your lunch bag. Can you memorize it on the way to school? Review the verse as you eat lunch. If you use a lunch box instead of a bag, tape a Bible memory card to your lunch box.

The Top 50

Here are 50 verses most likely to be memorized in a Bible memory program. They are not necessarily the most important verses in the Bible. But they are frequently memorized. A summary statement of each verse is given:

1. God created the universe. *(Genesis 1:1)*

2. Honor your parents. *(Exodus 20:12)*

3. Don't steal. *(Exodus 20:15)*

4. Don't lie. *(Exodus 20:16)*

5. Choose to follow God. *(Joshua 24:15)*

6. Your God will be my God. *(Ruth 1:16)*

7. God looks on the heart, not on outward appearance. *(1 Samuel 16:7)*

8. If God's people turn from their sin, He will hear them. *(2 Chronicles 7:14)*

9. The heavens declare God's glory. *(Psalm 19:1)*

10. The Lord is my Shepherd. *(Psalm 23:1)*

11. Create a clean heart in me, Lord. *(Psalm 51:10)*

12. God's Word is a light to my feet. *(Psalm 119:105)*

13. Teach a child how to go, and he will continue that way. *(Proverbs 22:6)*

14. Remember God while you are young. *(Ecclesiastes 12:1)*

15. Grass dies and flowers fade, but God's Word is forever. *(Isaiah 40:8)*

16. Look for the Lord while you can find Him. *(Isaiah 55:6)*

17. I ate your words, and they fed my soul. *(Jeremiah 15:16)*

18. Call on me and I will answer you. *(Jeremiah 33:3)*

19. When God's people help others come to Him they are like the stars forever. *(Daniel 12:3)*

20. Whatever you want others to do, do first to them. *(Matthew 7:12)*

21. Jesus is God's Son who came to seek and save the lost. *(Matthew 18:11)*

22. Let the little children come to Me. *(Matthew 19:14)*

23. I am with you always. *(Matthew 28:20)*

24. To get into God's kingdom, you must come as a little child. *(Mark 10:15)*

25. Give and it will be given to you. *(Luke 6:38)*

26. Give us this day our daily bread. *(Luke 11:3)*

27. God loved the world so much that He gave His son. *(John 3:16)*

28. I am the Good Shepherd. *(John 10:11)*

29. I am the Resurrection and the Life. *(John 11:25)*

30. I am the Way, the Truth and the Life. *(John 14:6)*

31. If you love me, obey me. *(John 14:15)*

32. Believe in the Lord Jesus Christ and you will be saved. *(Acts 16:31)*

33. You are the temple of God. *(1 Corinthians 3:16)*

34. If any one is in Christ he is a new creation.
    (2 Corinthians 5:17)

35. If you give little you receive little... God loves a cheerful
    giver. *(2 Corinthians 9:6-7)*

36. The fruit of the Spirit. *(Galatians 5:22-23)*

37. Children, obey your parents. *(Ephesians 6:1)*

38. Put on the whole armor of God. *(Ephesians 6:11)*

39. Let this mind be in you that was in Christ. *(Philippians
    2:5)*

40. At the name of Jesus every knee shall bow. *(Philippians
    2:10)*

41. Obey your father and mother. *(Colossians 3:20)*

42. In everything give thanks. *(1 Thessalonians 5:18)*

43. What you have heard, teach others. *(2 Timothy 2:2)*

44. Study to show yourself approved. *(2 Timothy 2:15)*

45. Come boldly to the throne of grace. *(Hebrews 4:16)*

46. Jesus is the same yesterday, today, and forever. *(Hebrews
    13:8)*

47. Cast all your cares upon Him. *(1 Peter 5:7)*

48. Love not the world, nor things in the world. *(1 John
    2:15)*

49. I stand at the door and knock. *(Revelation 3:20)*

50. God will wipe all tears from their eyes. *(Revelation 21:4)*

Memory Plus

For those who want to memorize more, here is some of the most important Bible memory work, beyond the key verses, that you can do:

The Books of the Bible

The Ten Commandments *(Exodus 20: 3-17)*

The Twelve Sons of Jacob—and thus the twelve tribes of Israel *(Genesis 35:22-26)*

The Shepherd Psalm *(Psalm 23)*

The Twelve Disciples *(Matthew 10: 2-4; Mark 3:14-19; Luke 6:13-16; Acts 1:13)*

The Beatitudes *(Matthew 5:3-12)*

The Lord's Prayer *(Matthew 6:9-13; Luke 11:2-4)*

The Golden Rule *(Luke 6:31)*

The Great Love Chapter *(1 Corinthians 13)*

The Fruit of the Spirit *(Galatians 5:22-23)*

God's Armor *(Ephesians 6:10-17)*

Bible Memory Topics

The following are Bible memory topics in this book, with Bible teachings and references:

ANGER: Answer angry words with kind ones. *(Proverbs 15:1)*

ANGER: Control your anger. *(Proverbs 14:29)*

ANGER: You are wise when you control your anger. *(Proverbs 29:11)*

BAD THINGS: Say no to bad things or you will get into trouble. *(James 1:15)*

BAD WORDS: Be careful what you say. *(James 3:5)*

BAD WORDS: Don't say things that will get you into trouble. *(Proverbs 21:23)*

BAD WORDS: Watch what you say. *(Psalm 34:13)*

BEAUTY: God made a beautiful creation. *(Ecclesiastes 3:11)*

BEAUTY: God is a beautiful Person. *(Psalm 27:4)*

BEAUTY: God says we are beautiful if we have a good heart. *(1 Samuel 16:7)*

BEAUTY: Sharing God's Good News makes us more beautiful. *(Isaiah 52:7)*

BEST: Do your best. *(Ecclesiastes 9:10)*

BEST: You will be glad when you do your best. *(Galatians 6:4)*

BIBLE: Reading the Bible will give you joy. *(Jeremiah 15:16)*

BIBLE: Memorizing God's Word will keep me from sinning. *(Psalm 119:11)*

BIBLE: Obey God's Word. *(Luke 11:28)*

BIBLE: I should memorize the Bible to be able to remember it when I have a need. *(Psalm 119:16)*

BIBLE: I should memorize the Bible to learn where to go. *(Psalm 119:105)*

CARE: Be careful what you say. *(James 3:5)*

CHEERFULNESS: Give cheerfully. *(2 Corinthians 9:7)*

CHILDREN: Help a child choose the right path. *(Proverbs 22:6)*

CHOOSING: God will teach me what is best. *(Psalm 25:12)*

CHOOSING: There is a right time for everything. *(Ecclesiastes 3:1)*

CHOOSING: Help a child choose the right path. *(Proverbs 22:6)*

CONTROL: You are wise when you control your anger. *(Proverbs 29:11)*

CONTROL: Control your anger. *(Proverbs 14:29)*

CREATION: We should rejoice because God made our day. *(Psalm 118:24)*

CREATION: God made a beautiful creation. *(Ecclesiastes 3:11)*

DOING: Do your best. *(Ecclesiastes 9:10)*

EXAMPLE: Set a good example by doing good. *(Titus 2:7)*

EXAMPLE: Do what Jesus would do. *(1 Corinthians 11:1)*

EXAMPLE: Set a good example by what you say and do. *(1 Timothy 4:12)*

FAITHFULNESS: Jesus will be with you always. *(Matthew 28:20)*

FORGIVING: God wants to forgive us. *(Psalm 86:5)*

FORGIVING: We should forgive each other. *(Ephesians 4:32)*

FRIENDSHIP: Jesus wants you to be His friend. *(John 15:14)*

GENEROSITY: Give generously. *(Deuteronomy 16:17)*

GIVING: Give part of all you get. *(1 Corinthians16:2)*

GIVING: Give cheerfully. *(2 Corinthians 9:7)*

GIVING: Give generously. *(Deuteronomy 16:17)*

GLADNESS: You will be glad when you do your best. *(Galatians 6:4)*

GODLY: To be godly and holy is to be peaceful and quiet. *(1 Timothy 2:2)*

GOD'S WAY: God will teach me what is best. *(Psalm 25:12)*

GOD'S WAY: Help a child choose the right path. *(Proverbs 22:6)*

GOD'S WORD: I should memorize the Bible to show me where to go. *(Psalm 119:105)*

GOD'S WORD: Memorizing God's Word will keep me from sinning. *(Psalm 119:11)*

GOD'S WORD: Obey God's Word. *(Luke 11:28)*

GOD'S WORD: I should memorize God's Word to remember it. *(Psalm 119:16)*

HELPING: Helping God will give you joy. *(Psalm 100:2)*

HELPING: Being kind to others helps us too. *(Proverbs 11:17)*

HELPING: We should help each other. *(Isaiah 41:6)*

HELPING: The Lord helps us. (Psalm 118:13)

HELPING: We should help those who need us. *(Galatians 2:10)*

HONOR: We honor God when we are kind to poor people. *(Proverbs 14:31)*

JOY: Our hearts and lips should rejoice together. *(Psalm 16:9)*

JOY: Helping God will give you joy. *(Psalm 100:2)*

JOY: You will find joy when God is with you. *(Psalm 35:9)*

JOY: Reading the Bible will give you joy. *(Jeremiah 15:16)*

JOY: We should rejoice in God all the time. *(Philippians 4:4)*

JOY: We should rejoice because God made our day. *(Psalm 118:24)*

KINDNESS: We honor God when we are kind to poor people. *(Proverbs 14:31)*

KINDNESS: We should be kind to others. *(Ephesians 4:32)*

KINDNESS: Answer angry words with kind ones. *(Proverbs 15:1)*

KINDNESS: Being kind to others helps us too. *(Proverbs 11:17)*

LOVE: Jesus wants you to love others as He loves you. *(John 15:12)*

LOVE: God loves us forever. *(Jeremiah 31:3)*

LOVE: Love each other. *(1 John 3:23)*

LOVE: Love God with all your heart. *(Matthew 22:37)*

LOVE: Jesus loves you. *(John 15:9)*

MEMORIZING: I should memorize the Bible to show me where to go. *(Psalm 119:105)*

MEMORIZING: Memorizing God's Word will keep me from sinning. *(Psalm 119:11)*

MEMORIZING: I should memorize the Bible to remember it. *(Psalm 119:16)*

NO: Don't listen when friends tempt you. *(Proverbs 1:10)*

NO: Say no to bad things, or you will get into trouble. *(James 1:15)*

NO: Ask God to help you say no. *(Ephesians 6:11)*

OBEY: Obey your parents. *(Ephesians 6:1)*

OBEY: Obey God's Word. *(Luke 11:28)*

OBEY: Obey God. *(Acts 5:29)*

OTHERS: Being kind to others helps us too. *(Proverbs 11:17)*

OTHERS: We should be kind to others. *(Ephesians 4:32)*

PARENTS: Obey your parents. *(Ephesians 6:1)*

PATIENCE: Patience keeps us from quarreling. *(Proverbs 15:18)*

PEACE: To be godly and holy is to be peaceful and quiet. *(1 Timothy 2:2)*

PEACE: Live peacefully with each other. *(1 Thessalonians 5:13)*

PEACE: Peacefulness comes from the Lord. *(Colossians 3:15)*

POOR: We honor God when we are kind to poor people. *(Proverbs 14:31)*

PRAYING: God hears and answers prayer. *(Jeremiah 33:3)*

PRAYING: When we pray, we are talking to God. *(Psalm 5:2)*

PRAYING: When you have trouble, pray. *(James 5:13)*

PRIDE: Pride causes us to quarrel. *(Proverbs 13:10)*

PRIDE: Hate pride because God hates pride. *(Proverbs 8:13)*

PRIDE: Pride causes a person to fall. *(Proverbs 16:18)*

QUARRELING: Patience keeps us from quarreling. *(Proverbs 15:18)*

QUARRELING: Pride causes us to quarrel. *(Proverbs 13:10)*

REJOICING: We should rejoice because God made our day. *(Psalm 118:24)*

REJOICING: Our hearts and lips should rejoice together. *(Psalm 16:9)*

REJOICING: We should rejoice in God all the time. *(Philippians 4:4)*

REMEMBER: I should memorize the Bible to remember it. *(Psalm 119:16)*

RIGHT: Help a child choose the right path. *(Proverbs 22:6)*

SELFISHNESS: Hate pride because God hates pride. *(Proverbs 8:13)*

SELFISHNESS: Follow God, not selfishness. *(Psalm 119:36)*

SHARING: Share as God has shared with you. *(Deuteronomy 16:17)*

SHARING: Follow God, not selfishness. *(Psalm 119:36)*

SHARING: God is pleased when we share. *(Hebrews 13:16)*

SIN: Memorizing God's Word will help keep you from sinning. *(Psalm 119:11)*

TEMPTATION: Ask God to help you say no. *(Ephesians 6:11)*

TEMPTATION: Don't listen when friends tempt you. *(Proverbs 1:10)*

TEMPTATION: Say no to bad things, or you will get into trouble. *(James 1:15)*

THANKS: God wants you always to be thankful. *(1 Thessalonians 5:18)*

THANKS: Be thankful. *(Colossians 3:15)*

THANKS: It is good to give thanks to the Lord. *(Psalm 92:1)*

TIME: There is a right time for everything. *(Ecclesiastes 3:1)*

TROUBLE: Don't say things that will get you into trouble. *(Proverbs 21:23)*

TROUBLE: When you have trouble, pray. *(James 5:13)*

WATCH: Watch what you say. *(Psalm 34:13)*

WISE: You are wise when you control your anger. *(Proverbs 29:11)*

WORDS: Be careful what you say. *(James 3:5)*

WORDS: Watch what you say. *(Psalm 34:13)*

WORDS: Don't say things that will get you into trouble. *(Proverbs 21:23)*

WORK: Work hard for God. *(2 Timothy 2:15)*

WORK: Work to please the Lord. *(Colossians 3:23)*

WORK: When you do any work, do it for the Lord. *(Colossians 3:23)*

WORRY: You should not worry. *(Matthew 6:25)*

WORRY: Worry will not help you. *(Matthew 6:27)*